Elinor Fitch Griffin, *Island of Childhood: Education
in the Special World of Nursery School*

Sandra R. Curtis, *The Joy of Movement in Early Childhood*

Frances E. Kendall, *Diversity in the Classroom:
A Multicultural Approach to the Education
of Young Children*

James T. Greenman and Robert W. Fuqua, editors,
*Making Day Care Better: Training, Evaluation,
and the Process of Change*

Evelyn Weber, *Ideas Influencing Early Childhood
Education: A Theoretical Analysis*

Constance Kazuko Kamii, *Young Children Reinvent
Arithmetic: Implications of Piaget's Theory*

Nancy Balaban, *Starting School: From Separation
to Independence (A Guide for Early Childhood Teachers)*

John Cleverley and D. C. Phillips, *Visions of Childhood:
Influential Models from Locke to Spock*

Joseph J. Caruso and M. Temple Fawcett, *Supervision
in Early Childhood Education: A Developmental Perspective*

Bernard Spodek, editor, *Today's Kindergarten:
Exploring the Knowledge Base, Expanding the Curriculum*

Margaret V. Yonemura, *A Teacher at Work: Professional
Development and the Early Childhood Educator*

A Teacher at Work

PROFESSIONAL DEVELOPMENT AND THE EARLY CHILDHOOD EDUCATOR

Margaret V. Yonemura

in collaboration with
Jean Acosta-Colletti and Jeffrey Collins

TEACHERS
COLLEGE
PRESS

Teachers College, Columbia University
New York and London

**To Myra and David, my earliest teachers,
and to Ariana, Lily, and Will, my latest teachers**

Published by Teachers College Press, 1234 Amsterdam Avenue,
New York, N.Y. 10027

Library of Congress Cataloging in Publication Data

Yonemura, Margaret V.
  A teacher at work.

  (Early childhood education series ; 11)
  Bibliography: p. 151
  Includes index.
  1. Education, Preschool—New York (N.Y.)—Case
studies. 2. Child psychology—Case studies. 3. Teacher–
student relationships—New York (N.Y.)—Case studies.
4. Nursery school teachers—New York (N.Y.)—Attitudes—
Case studies. 5. Laboratory schools—New York (N.Y.)—
Case studies. I. Acosta-Colletti, Jean. II. Collins,
Jeffrey. III. Title. IV. Series.
LB1140.245.N49Y67 1986   372'.21'097471 86-14363
ISBN 0-8077-2832-2
ISBN 0-8077-2815-2 (pbk.)

Manufactured in the United States of America

91 90 89 88 87 86   1 2 3 4 5 6

Contents

Preface

I share with many others a concern that those of us who work with young children, either directly as teachers or indirectly as administrators, improve our practice. We do influence lives, often powerfully, and, as many diverse sources remind us, not always optimally. We continue to neglect one potential source for developing our profession: those teachers among us who are performing at high levels of excellence. In three decades as an early childhood educator, I have met many. Unfortunately, their work goes largely undocumented. It influences those around them, but it does not reach the profession at large.

It seems important and urgent to record some of this effective, even superb practice and to think about the implications for professional development that emerge from studying such teaching.

I ask the reader to join me in putting aside for the moment the heady technological wings that enable us to see vast populations from Olympian heights in order to experience a close encounter with Jean—a teacher—and with the children and other adults in her classroom.

Much of the description and the implications of Jean's work revolve around values and beliefs, the pilot ships of teaching that determine which of many directions we choose to take. This study caused me to reflect deeply on values—what I believe, what I do, and aspects of who I am. I have found this professionally sustaining and renewing, and I hope no less for the readers who may find echoes of themselves and their own work with children reverberating in these pages.

The nature and demands of educating young children still go unrecognized for the most part, a situation that is reflected dramatically in the dismal salaries of many in the field. In describing in detail the dynamic, draining, intellectually alive world of one teacher, my voice, I hope, will join those of others in the profession in dismissing the belief that teaching young children is a simple affair. I would like to help build respect for the complexity of teaching when it is based on a view of young children as active searchers for meaning who are richly endowed with capacities that we have only recently begun to recognize and to celebrate those children as promises of what they will become.

Acknowledgments

My thanks go to my husband, George, who continues to illuminate for me the pilgrim's progress of professional development in the human services; to my daughter, Isobel, a committed member of the early childhood field with helpful new perspectives for me; and to my son-in-law, Jim Moir, for his probing, searching questions about what might be. Jean Acosta-Colletti and Jeffrey Collins, colleagues in the study, I rank with my best teachers, and I have been blessed with a generous number of those at Abbott House; Teachers College, Columbia University; Bank Street College of Education; Queens College, City University of New York; and the Susquehanna School. I would also like to thank Jane Connor, a faculty member in the Department of Psychology and Director of the nursery school at the State University of New York at Binghamton, for her ongoing cooperation. Nancy Ramirez and Lisa Dickerson, graduate students in the Division of Professional Education, and Julie Quinn, division secretary, have given invaluable as well as good-humored support. I am also indebted to Nina George of Teachers College Press, who has guided the book to its final form.

To Gloria Gaumer I express much appreciation for her patience and skill in typing the final manuscript. Through the offices of Dean James Votruba and Associate Dean Theodore Rector, and through interactions with my colleagues in the School of General Studies and Professional Education, I have received ideas, encouragement, and services to facilitate this work. I wish that others who work with young children might also receive such support in their endeavors.

Observation of a comet found in the spring of 1983 has increased astronomers' understanding of all comets.

—Stephen P. Maran, "Thereby Hangs a Tail,"
Natural History, June 1984

1 Studying One Effective Teacher

Sometimes, on our paths through school, we meet teachers who are special. Years later we remember them, able to trace an idea, an ambition, even an attitude, to our being with them. Few of us, however, can remember with clarity such teachers from our early years, although their influence, powerful despite its submergence in our unconscious, is widely acknowledged.

Descriptions are sparse about how such teachers go about their teaching and how their values and beliefs find expression in ways that educate children well. As part of the task of learning more about such effective teachers, this book centers on just one early childhood teacher. Her work is presented through the eyes of the teacher herself, Jean Acosta-Colletti; a teacher educator, Margaret Yonemura; and Jeffrey Collins, a student teacher in Jean's classroom.

Jean teaches in the laboratory school of the State University of New York at Binghamton. She is regarded as "a very good teacher" by her supervisor, a member of the Department of Psychology; by a wide range of undergraduate and graduate students in psychology and education; by the great majority of the parents of the 56 children whom she teaches; and by her peers in the local professional association to which she belongs. Each of these observers is impressed by different aspects of her teaching. Therefore, an outsider can piece together fragments of what makes her teaching work from a variety of perspectives. This book provides an inside look at Jean as a teacher, painting impressionistically and holistically some of the life in her classroom.

Before giving the reader this view of Jean's teaching, it must be acknowledged that there is no consensus on what constitutes teaching or who is agreed to be an effective teacher.

EFFECTIVE TEACHING

In a time of social upheaval, many look nostalgically back to a time when "teachers knew how to teach." Oliver Goldsmith, in his poem *The Deserted Village*, offers a record of the painful exodus of farm laborers from the country to the new factories and mills of industrial cities. Deprived of access to the land by the Enclosure Act, the villagers lost their livelihood, and the villages became empty shells. Reflecting on the time when they were thriving, Goldsmith describes one of the mainstays of these small societies, the village schoolmaster. Here was a leader none questioned and all respected:

> Amaz'd the gazing rustics rang'd around;
> And still they gaz'd, and still the wonder grew
> That one small head could carry all he knew.

A person of status and a valued member of his community, he was training subjects to live in a monarchy where obedience to a rigid class system was essential, a no-nonsense society where theft of a sheep could mean death. The knowledge he held in his head was not there to be shared equally with his pupils; only enough of it was to be imparted to give them a proper respect for what was in his head and the heads of "their betters." He was not interested in educating citizens for a democracy, ready to question right and wrong in society, ready to tackle difficult intellectual ideas and respond humanely to unpredictable societal changes, ready to confront the challenge of maintaining and adding to what is beautiful in the world.

In other words, his teaching was back to basics and nothing more. Society dictated his role, spelled it out clearly; he fulfilled it and was rewarded by the approval of the authorities. His role was clear-cut, unambiguous, and visible to all. The high level of accountability of his role as a teacher was a logical outgrowth of the society in which he lived, as was the concept of school knowledge to be conveyed. Today teachers are held accountable by a variety of constituencies, sometimes with different expectations, and teachers themselves hold different values and beliefs about the nature of education. Some choose to act as if knowledge were a commodity funneled through or parceled out by them. Others view human beings as basically endowed with capacities to gain and generate knowledge that all healthy individuals use, so that there are no empty vessels. Teaching becomes a mutual enterprise in which the knowledge of young learners of all ages is valued and is put to work as a means of extending the understanding of all involved in the teaching-learning process. In contemporary society, effectiveness eludes easy definition, and it is hoped that the nature of Jean's particular kind of effectiveness as a teacher will emerge as this book develops.

The reader may wonder about the need to know more about effective teaching and, in particular, why the decision was made to invest considerable time and energy in the study of one teacher. There has been much research on effective teaching, but, until recently, it has focused on the direct observables of teaching, such as the questions asked or the movements of the teacher in the classroom. Attention has been paid to the parts of teaching—the ability to plan, to make countless decisions on one's feet, to ask a range of questions, and to make careful observations. We have learned a great deal about teaching through such quantifiable, empirical-analytic research, but we have not learned how these parts fuse into a synergetic whole. The cellist Yo-Yo Ma was once asked to give his opinion of Pablo Casals' exquisite interpretation of Bach. He pointed out that the beauty lay not in one note he played but in the combination of notes. Similarly with teaching, adding up the "notes" or parts only partially reveals its effectiveness. How the parts combine into a unified whole must be considered. A way of presenting a holistic, qualitative view of teaching is needed to complement the quantitative observables in order to understand its complexity more fully.

VALUES AND BELIEFS

There is more to teaching than meets the senses, and this includes the feelings, ideas, values, beliefs, and intentions and other unseen but present territory of the minds of children and teachers. In one classroom, the terrarium is a locus for children to observe, record, explore, control, spend time watching the teacher demonstrate, question, and engage in scientific inquiry. In another classroom, the teacher talks to the children about the terrarium and later questions them to see if they are accumulating facts. The children in both classrooms can be observed overtly in relation to the terraria, but the ideas and beliefs of the teachers in relation to a science curriculum influence the children's experience differently in the long run.

Inquiry focused upon effective teaching has to move beyond surface observables into teachers' minds. An excellent start in this direction was made by Bussis, Chittenden and Amarel (1976), who interviewed and observed elementary school teachers in what were labeled open education classrooms. They spent much time finding out what the teachers believed and saw how these beliefs were or were not implemented in the classroom. Some teachers were effective and some were not, but what is crucial to note is that the least effective and most anxious teachers really did not believe in what they were doing. They did not understand the reasons for what they did and were not committed to what they were doing—in contrast to those teachers judged effective, who held values and beliefs consistent with the underlying constructs of open education.

To understand more about effective teachers, it is imperative to know more about their thinking—their ideas, values, and beliefs, how consistently they are put into practice, and the meaning this has for the children. In this study of Jean's work, the focus was upon the area of values and beliefs. Another area intrigued us that, at the end of the study, we felt we were barely beginning to grasp. We wanted to explore together the neglected domain of teachers' practical knowledge, which has too long been relegated to the frequently gender-linked, untouchable realm of the intuitive.

A WEALTH OF HIDDEN KNOWLEDGE

Caroline Pratt (1948) believed that young children stored within themselves a hidden wealth of knowledge. Piaget's work has supplied evidence of the dynamic evolving structures that help to create this knowledge from birth onward. Surely, teachers are no less rich epistemologically than the children they teach. Like them, and in common with other adults who remain learners, teachers have a hidden wealth of knowledge out of which emerges the practical knowledge that guides them consciously and intuitively in the countless decisions of teaching. Studies of this practical knowledge could extend our knowledge of teaching, shed more light on the mesh between the espoused values and beliefs of effective teachers and the actual enactment of their teaching, and begin to unravel the meaning of all this for the classroom lives of the children.

Practical knowledge is not confined to professional life. We draw on it when we plan our vacations. It would seem uncommonly pompous to announce that we have a theory about planning a vacation. However, a moment taken to think about it will dignify the set of assumptions, hypotheses, and aspirations for the future that go into such theorizing about an everyday event (Argyris & Schon, 1975). Some of us are very effective at such planning, while others muddle along. So it is in teaching, medicine, law, and other professions. The complete activities of minutes, days, and larger time units do not flow unguided from the teacher's head. When 4-year-old Jill bites 4-year-old Lorna on the arm, something has to be done at once. Intuitively, teachers know what to do, and values and beliefs play a part in determining how the biting is understood—whether it is seen as immoral and needing to be punished, viewed as related to the setting and environmental conditions, or seen as a combination of these or other causes. Understandings derived from such disciplines as psychology and anthropology may find a place in the teacher's conjecturing about and responding to the meaning of the biting because the practice of professionals is supported by a body of formal knowledge derived from the disciplines. But the disciplines neither separately nor together make claim to give the answers to the complexity of teaching. The teacher draws on a reservoir of experiences woven into strategies for responding to the new scenarios provided everyday in the classroom. It is the values and beliefs of the teacher that play an important part in which strategies out of many possible are selected.

Many complex, interacting thoughts help us select one path among a potential myriad. These thoughts often come like lightning, not in linear sequence. But they are thoughts, and they are not random. We may be unable to explain them, but through reflection we may come to a better understanding of them. Practical knowledge is a guide for action, and it is important to recognize that it is underpinned by values and beliefs that, for better or for worse, influence children's lives.

Yet much of this practical knowledge is held implicitly, unavailable for conscious assessment. Those engaged in professional development have no formal body of knowledge that reveals the knowledge amalgam derived from a combination of professional studies with teachers' own practical knowledge, as Elbaz (1981) has pointed out. Even more serious, teachers' actions in the classroom often go unexplored for the hidden assumptions and untested hypotheses growing out of this amalgam. Without access to more of the thinking that underlies teaching, its deep structure is lost to us, and we compensate by drenching ourselves in surface observables.

Surface behaviors alone are superficial. Virginia Woolf (1976) wrote of the futility of writing life stories if one could not identify the "invisible presences" influencing one's life, close relatives, certain public opinions, and other significant persons and events. When these remain implicit, she said, "I see myself as a fish in a stream; deflected; held in place; but cannot describe the stream" (p. 80). McDermott (1982) put this less poetically than Woolf, but equally powerfully, when he wrote, "Immersed in water, an ethnographer should come out with the skills of a swimmer and a hydrologist" (p. 322).

As professionals many of us feel ourselves deflected at times by a stream of events that leave us bewildered because we cannot grasp their composition. In this study, the decision was made to stem the flow of Jean's teaching long enough to understand its nature better, in the hope that it would begin to reveal its "invisible presences" and that we would become more aware of its hidden sources.

As Jeff and I observed Jean and later talked with her about what she did, we both gained a great respect for her practical knowledge. She seemed to know just when to move in to the play, when to cut short on group meeting time, when to make an exception to a rule. Almost always she could give an account of the thought that led her to these actions, and these thoughts could be traced back to values and beliefs.

I do not feel that I have done justice to Jean's practical knowledge, but I feel strongly that no adequate description of an effective teacher can ignore this. We have a long history, influenced by the reductionism of behaviorism to view teachers as black boxes or as the "cultural dopes" met as the subjects or informants of earlier studies in anthropology (Erickson, 1979). Contempt for the practical wisdom of teachers can be inferred from their exclusion as partners in many curriculum projects of the sixties and seventies, in which scholars in the disciplines sometimes designed programs without consulting classroom teachers. The failure of many such projects has been well documented (Sarason, 1971). The neglect of teachers' practical knowledge weakens the profession.

ONE EARLY CHILDHOOD EDUCATOR

Because of the need for more knowledge about effective teaching, a study of this kind, focusing on just one teacher, seemed warranted. This in-depth study of Jean's teaching, its meaning to her, and how she understood the events of the day and the lives of the children is phenomenological in nature, justified not as a replacement for empirical-analytic studies but as a complement. Cassirer (1970) said, "It is characteristic of the nature of man that he is not limited to one specific and single approach to reality but can choose his point of view and so pass from one aspect of things to another" (p. 188). It seemed to us appropriate to pass from the surface of teaching to enter its depths, spending time and energy on Jean's work.

Margaret Mead (1972) described how her intense observation and relationship with her grandchild, 2-year-old Vanni, gave her new eyes to bring to all 2-year-olds: "When Vanni is present, I see the children around her with greater clarity; when she is not there, I visualize 2-year-olds—all the 2-year-olds—with new comprehension. I see their faces more clearly" (p. 282). Through her immersion in the world of Vanni, Mead felt a deepening of her ability to understand and care for all children.

Immersion in the work of one teacher holds similar promise for deepening understanding of other teachers, opening up new perspectives and sharpening existing ones, perhaps raising new questions, and refocusing on questions that have been with us in teaching for a long time. To explore this promise, Jean and I decided together to spend a year studying her teaching and the thinking, values, and beliefs underlying her practice and to trace their impact on the growth and development on the 14 young children she taught. We were both committed to the importance of knowing more about the practical knowledge that guides teaching, Jean's focus being her own professional development and mine being a general concern, as a teacher educator, with ways of supporting professional development more effectively.

Jean's responsibilities as a teacher were broad, involving the supervision of students in field placements in psychology and education courses and of assistant teachers, as well as planning and administering programs for 56 children. The children were divided into four groups that used the same classroom at different times of the week. Her role and its enactment qualify her to be described as "an early childhood educator, a 'double specialist' working with children and adults on many complex levels" (Almy, 1975, p. 28). From observing and interacting with her over several years, I had gathered fragments of the store of formal and practical knowledge that guided her teaching, about which she was unusually reflective. We were very interested in uncovering more of this invisible but powerful base of her professional life. The procedures we followed are discussed below. In brief, we engaged in taped conversations about her teaching and made direct observations of her classroom.

PROCEDURES

In our quest to understand Jean's teaching more fully, we found a partner, Jeff, a student teacher in the master's education program who had been in Jean's room as a psychology undergraduate assistant teacher in the spring semester in 1982. He was going to be given much greater responsibility for the group in the fall of 1982. An experienced teacher's induction of a novice seemed a likely time for formal and informal theories as well as espoused values to surface. Jeff agreed to having Jean's supervisory conferences with him in the fall of 1982 taped. My weekly conferences with Jean were taped in the spring. These were seen as data rich in potential for mining Jean's beliefs and values.

Jean was neither a subject nor a respondent nor a case but a coresearcher filling the role described by Spradley (1979) of the informant in some ethnographic research "as one who is not studied but is a person from whom the researcher, in the traditional usage of the term, learns and acts" (p. 34). In effect, Jean and I acted as teachers to each other much as Smith and Geoffrey (1968) did in the study reported in *The Complexities of an Urban Classroom*. Smith, a university investigator, sat in Geoffrey's inner-city seventh-grade classroom for 80% of a semester. He acted as a participant observer, taking notes and reflecting on them. Geoffrey also made notes of the events of the day and his perspective on them. The authors noted that this was the first time educational research had utilized the perspectives of a university investigator and classroom teacher.

I took Dilthey's (1977) advice when he said that we miss too much if we insist on treating the study of trees and human beings in the same way. We will never know what trees are experiencing as they live, grow, develop, and die, but we can know what our fellows experience if we take the time to listen. I have tried to search out the meanings behind events, rejecting treating Jean or the children as "subjects" without inner lives. I have also tried to immerse myself in Jean's world, to see it through her eyes and to avoid inserting my own meaning prematurely. When an event seemed puzzling to me I have tried to remember that "human beings act toward things on the basis of the meanings that the things have for them" (Blumer, 1969, p. 2), an axiom long held in the field of early childhood education.

We recognized that our reflections together on her teaching must be balanced by observations of the events of the classroom. To check our tendencies to reduce complexities to banalities, we needed to dip back and catch as much of the wealth of ongoing life as we could. So much of teacher talk about teaching is telegraphed into messages that do not do justice to the endeavor. A teacher speaking of a child will encapsulate all the complete interactions of group work and educational programming in the phrase "gets along well with his peers." Teachers are not alone in this tendency to reduce the complex to a simple, less rich formulation.

Schachtel (1947/1968) warned that even the most exciting events are remembered as milestones rather than as moments filled with the concrete abundance of life: "Adult memory reflects life as a road with occasional signposts and milestones rather than as the landscape through which the road has led" (p. 18). We remember what everyone is supposed to remember, what everyone remembers, and the unique stamp of our own experience is lost. Bored, we experience events in a stereotypic way. Schachtel found confirmation of this tendency in the studies of F. C. Bartlett (1932), in which subjects were shown photographs of men in the armed services, both naval and army officers and men in rank. They were asked to describe them 30 minutes later, one week later, and even later. The descriptions changed progressively with time in the direction of the conventional, becoming less and less faithful to the original.

Memories of teaching similarly became more stereotypic, less differentiated, and far less interesting when they are fitted into and disrobed by limiting, containing clichés. As one teacher put it, "When I'm asked about my teaching, I play the same record for many people. I find myself giving a pat answer." These pat answers reflect a concern Maslow (1968) shared with Schachtel about our tendency "to rubricize," to pigeonhole persons and events before we have seen their uniqueness. Categorization is an invaluable capacity of mind, helping us deal economically with many data, thus making them manageable. However, when it is perpetual or premature, it can lead to creating a wholly predictable, static universe in which new, vivid perspectives and understandings are lost. We recognized that going back to raw experience and trying to see Jean's teaching holistically, to grasp it in fresh, more productive ways, would be no easy task. The refreshment of a new view and the potential for an added dimension to our work were seen as justification enough for the efforts. As Jean Miller (1976) has pointed out:

> The closer the mind can connect with what it is actually experiencing, the better its inherent creativity can flourish. The more opportunity we have to put our mental creations into action, the more comprehensively we can, in turn, feel and think. One builds on the other. (p. 112)

My own work took me to the nursery school on a regular informal basis all year, but I formally observed Jean in her classroom one morning a week for one and a half hours for 10 weeks in the spring in order to make running records of her interaction with individual children, with small groups, and with the total group. The running records were an attempt to grasp raw experience out of which we could infer aspects of her beliefs and practical knowledge. Observations were the starting points and served to structure but not limit the conferences. They often led to reminiscences of past events in the classroom, richly detailed because of Jean's keen powers of observation and retentive memory. The children's works, the paintings and songs they learned, the games they played, the buildings they made, all provided further documentation of her teaching (Almy & Genishi, 1979).

The end product of running records is a collection of notes that must be interpreted. These lack the consoling precision of rating sheets and other useful, but also limiting, instruments. Trying to grasp teaching holistically through going back to raw experience can be overwhelming. The volume of data is intimidating. Writing about Clyfford Still's enormous abstract oil paintings, Katharine Kuh (1979) says, "twenty years ago the critic Kenneth Rexroth wrote, 'People came up to his vast pictures very quietly, toppled over into them without a murmur and came out with nothing to say'" (p. 12). Sometimes after observing a classroom for a morning, I have had the same sense of loss of words, of being absorbed by the complexity and depth of the experience. We are so used to the empirical-analytic mode that it is hard for us to deal with experience except by chopping it up into observable fragments to be counted. And yet holistic experience needs to be acknowledged, valued, and described if, as Eisner (1979) says, we are to better understand teaching.

INTRODUCING OURSELVES

Neither Jean, Jeff, nor I claim or wish to be value-free video machines. What we selected to record reflects our own values and beliefs and experiences. The reader may find it helpful to put these in perspective if we first introduce ourselves.

Jean

Jean sees her life as somewhat typical of the generation raised by parents who had grown up during the Depression and always wanted to give their children what they themselves never had. With upward socioeconomic mobility came vacations, TV, parochial school, store-bought clothes, and more toys than could have filled a toy box. It is only now, in her early thirties, that she is beginning to understand, appreciate, and try to pass on what they gave that money did not buy.

When she began college on a part-time basis, her interests were in biological sciences. However, she was raising an infant at the same time, and her concerns, responsibilities, and fascination in the development of this person became intriguing. In her first course, Literature for Young Children, she learned about language, its significance, and how it could influence her child's learning. Reading a bedtime story was no longer confined to Golden Books and Walt Disney. This course also became significant, for the professor soon became her advisor and engaged her in conversations about children and learning. She changed her major to nursery school education.

Watching her daughter grow day by day stirred endless thoughts, curiosity, and interest. *Play* became a word she needed to redefine. The impact of day-by-day experiences became apparent. She wanted to influence, yet she didn't want to cast in stone, for it was the child's spontaneity, curiosity, and imagination that she found so fascinating. How could she, as a parent, provide and create an environment that would nurture and enrich? As she began taking education classes, reading, and practicum, these interests followed and influenced her approach to teaching.

After attaining her associate degree in nursery education, she continued for a bachelor's degree. Her experiences varied as she observed and participated in nursery schools, Head Start centers, day care, an infant center, and grades kindergarten through 6. In all, she was allowed great freedom, flexibility, and support. Her first teaching position in a nursery school afforded her the same environment. In addition, she team taught half a day with Nancy, a teacher who at the time had 8 years of experience. From her Jean learned the nature of a collegial relationship. After 3½ years of working together they both resigned from their positions owing to external administrative "orders" regarding changes Jean's colleague had to make within the school. These orders, in their opinion, would have created a situation to the detriment of the educational program and raised safety issues. Jean still remembers how hard it was meeting with the parents on that day, and telling them that she had decided to resign. She had strong principles, and now it was time to defend them publicly. The personal and professional support she received from her colleague and the parents she worked with enabled her to act on this trying decision. It was also during this time that she asked her daughter what she thought about having a working mother. Her response was, "I think it's good that you're a teacher, because teaching is really an important job."

Her next teaching position came after relocating in another state. The challenge of working in the child study center described in this book was invigorating as well as exhausting. She worked at unusual positions: first as head teacher and 2 years later as head teacher and educational coordinator. The next year she found herself head teacher, educational coordinator, and associate director—she was the entire hierarchy. The challenge of developing the program, working with undergraduate and graduate students each year, has greatly influenced her interests in professional development.

During this time she pursued her master's degree on a part-time basis. It was then that she met Margaret. As she looks back on her experiences, she senses a nurturing of her professional development by those who share a humanistic ideology. Although she continually finds herself wanting and searching for knowledge to fill the cracks, she considers her professional experiences to be rich and fulfilling, largely due to a handful of professionals who have had tremendous impact on her teaching. She has come to value the importance of defensible principles and the courage to continually challenge what she believes. This attitude has been passed on to her, and she hopes to pass it on to other teachers.

After working in a classroom for nearly 9 years, she is considering further study. To pursue professional growth, and in turn the education of children, is a value that she hopes to pass on to others which has been nurtured in her and in another teacher.

Jeff

Jeff was born in a small town in central New York and raised in a nurturing environment of six older siblings. His parents devoted most of their time and energy to the raising of their children. He found it difficult to separate from this happy setting when the time came for him to begin school.

Jeff's school years were characterized by numerous academic successes, though through high school his social life continued to center on his family. Indeed, academic proficiency often became a basis for social contacts, for he was always eager to help others with schoolwork. This interest has continued throughout his life.

His first job experience dealing with children was summer playground supervision. The children's ages ranged from 5 to 16, and with no training program, minimal staff support, and unenthusiastic coworkers, the job provided little impetus to counselor development, but he felt that he had some positive experiences and was learning.

The university's undergraduate courses dealing with children interested him, and he took as many as possible, fortunate that requirements for psychology majors left ample room for exploration. He learned about youth work, children's literature, and research in education, and had a public school internship. Finally, he hit on an even greater opportunity: the preschool directed by Jean.

This experimental preschool was a part of his own psychology department, most of which was heavily research-oriented. The many large, impersonal classes had left him cold, and now, as his interest in working with children increased, he began to seek a more precise focus on what he wanted. After spending a year in the research end of the preschool, Jeff became an assistant teacher.

Here he was happy with the great deal of thought that went into the teachers' interactions with children and with the support provided to them. His knowledge and enthusiasm swelled, and another important connection was made: He took an undergraduate course (offered by the graduate education department at the State University of New York at Binghamton), the purpose of which was "to determine whether teaching is for you."

Jeff began to feel that teaching *was* for him. The more he worked in classrooms, the more he was intrigued and the more he sought to learn. Jeff entered the university education department as a master's candidate, and feels it has been a great impetus in his life toward learning and meaning. Working closely with Jean, Margaret, and other skilled professionals, he has come to see both the practical and the theoretical sides of a great intellectual calling: helping children develop to their fullest potential.

Margaret

Margaret has spent about 30 years working with young children and those who raise and educate them. Growing up in Wales as an only child, when she was 12 she was joined by two 5-year-old foster sisters, World War II evacuees. She will never forget the influx to her small town of children who had left their families—their strength and resilience, the hard reunions and partings when families met again for brief periods. In undergraduate school, she studied social sciences at the University of London and became a social worker. Once again she saw children under difficult life circumstances in the slums of Bristol and London somehow evidencing vitality and intelligence. She remembers the times that the groups of children she was meant to lead took the lead from her, especially the one great game of netball that the girls did not want to end, although the clock said it was time, so they locked her out of the building. She learned to respect them and to want to win their respect but had no idea how this would come about.

In her early twenties, she came to the United States on a visit, and stayed to work as a counselor in a research hospital for children with rheumatic fever. Here she met her future husband. A brief period as a social caseworker with the children, a few home visits, and many conversations with their parents opened up the many dimensions and hazards of being poor in the world's most affluent society. Her respect for the coping abilities of the poor continued to grow. She began to sense that educating young children was her vocation, not "out of the blue" but as a natural outcome of those childhood years of playing school, of being with a schoolteacher father who loved his work and talked of "school" and "the boys," and at the drop of a hat would teach Welsh and English literature to anyone within hearing, quoting at length in sonorous tones the volumes stored in his retentive memory.

Following a year of full-time study at Teachers College, Columbia University, in the preservice master's program, Margaret fell into setting up, teaching, and directing a small program for the children in institutional care who filled the places of the rheumatic fever patients cured by the wonder drug penicillin. The program grew to include about 40 children between the ages of 2 and 7 years. A number of the children had handicapping conditions, but the majority were resilient inner-city children uprooted from their homes and families, broken under the conditions that go hand in hand with poverty. The 9 years spent directing the school were very rich, confirming for her the complex strengths children bring to making sense and meaning of lives under the worst conditions our society imposes.

Her graduate professional studies whetted Margaret's appetite for more, and she returned to complete a doctorate. Following this, she joined the faculty of Queens College, where she directed the laboratory school for children who came to school from middle-class homes for the most part. She was reminded that being middle-class does not bring a carefree existence—divorce, illness, death, and the press for upward mobility for the children bring other pressures. In this setting she worked closely with parents, as she had in social work, and shared closely their satisfaction and concerns in child raising. She found herself once again with lively, inquiring children, this time in a carefully designed setting with a staff at the master's level and a history of curriculum design and development.

After a decade of working with children in schools, Margaret made a full-time commitment to the graduate professional education of teachers, engaging in this at Teachers College, Columbia University; Queens College, City University of New York; Bank Street College of Education; and, for the past 11 years, State University of New York at Binghamton. She has had the chance to work closely with teachers and supervisors, children and parents, in all kinds of settings: rural, urban, and suburban.

The professional development of teachers and the education of young children were her major concerns. She wanted to use her experiences with Jean, a supervising teacher in a nursery school, and with Jeff, a master's student in professional education, to learn more about teaching and to document some of the processes she saw fostering their professional development. In doing so, her own development was furthered. Why Jean and Jeff? That they were there and willing was not enough in itself. By all indices we use (such as evaluation by peers, faculty, parents, grades, and tests), they ranked among the best. Margaret believed it was essential to know more about effective teachers— their values, beliefs, and thinking. She was concerned that too much education might not be educative at all, because teachers were held back from becoming professionals and steered into technician roles.

PLAN OF THE BOOK

Individual values and beliefs are not easily separated from the matrix in which they are embedded. Nevertheless, in the next three chapters an attempt is made to sort them out, although there is some overlapping.

In Chapter 2, Jean's beliefs about children are presented, after the reader has been introduced briefly to the setting and the children. In Chapter 3, Jean's perspectives on teaching are explored, and in Chapter 4, the focus is on her views of a sound educational program for young children. Chapter 5 looks at the impact of these values and beliefs upon the ongoing lives of the children. In all these chapters, conversations and running records provide evidence of the influence of Jean's values and beliefs on life in her classroom.

Jean's values and beliefs are shared by many in early childhood education. Even so, there are hurdles to practicing them, and these are discussed in Chapter 6. The book concludes with some implications suggested by this study of one effective early childhood teacher for ways to support the professional development of teachers and other human service professionals.

2 Jean's Beliefs About Children

Just as teaching is seen from a variety of perspectives, so are children viewed in different ways by both early childhood educators and the public. In this chapter some of Jean's most strongly held beliefs about children are presented, illustrated with examples of how they were enacted. First, a brief overview of the classroom and the children is provided.

THE SETTING

The nursery school classroom, with its one-way mirror, as described earlier, served both as an educational setting and as a laboratory for observation of the children, who were interviewed and tested periodically as part of psychological research projects. Jeff described it as follows:

> The classroom is of adequate, though not ample, size and is divided roughly into sections by activity areas. On the left, after a small front room, are the children's cubbies, in a row. Beyond this is the block area where there are shelves with blocks and various small toys, including cars and trucks. At the other corner is the circle of carpet squares on which the children sit for group discussion, with the teacher in a chair in the corner. Also, along the end wall is the flannel board, with boxes of various shapes and colors of felt. Beyond the circle is the long wall with the observation mirror and shelves with puzzles, small toys, and blocks of various types. These shelves extend into the room and, on the other side, a partially enclosed area is used for dress-up materials and the science corner.
>
> Beyond this, extending to the sink in the corner, is a small table, surrounded by a play stove, refrigerator, and sink, holding small dishes and water toys. Next to this is the

water table and on the other side of the room are easels for painting. At the end of the room there are the oven, cooking utensils, and shelves containing such items as paper, paint, glue, and scissors. In the middle of the room at the end are two large tables used for snacks, group activities, or table work and a fairly large round table used mainly for messier activities such as working with Play-Doh. The floor space at the other end of the room is largely open.

Completing the room are the pets—'Thumper' (the rabbit's cage being just to the right of the door) and the tropical fish (the aquarium being just above the rabbit's cage)—and the display table just behind the teacher's chair at the circle, featuring plants and any natural objects children bring to school: nests, bugs, and so forth. The room is brightly painted, which relieves to some degree the problems of windowless space, since this classroom is in the basement.

In one week, Jean worked with 56 children divided into four groups whose ages ranged from 3 to 5, each group attending for two half-day sessions weekly. As head teacher, she supervised in each group a male and female assistant teacher, who were undergraduate psychology majors. (Jeff acted as an assistant teacher in spring 1982.) Jean held weekly seminars for the eight psychology undergraduates and several graduate students in education whom she supervised in child study or graduate student teaching placements. Jeff acted as her graduate student teacher in fall 1982, when the study began.

One class of the four was selected for study because of time and energy limitations. It was made up of nine boys and five girls, with an age range in September of 3 through 5 years, eight of the children being 3. Two of the children,* Mickey and Peggy, were special education students who had been mainstreamed and were living in foster homes. In addition to being in Jean's class, both children attended a special education class. The services available for these young children were minimally coordinated, leaving Mickey and Peggy to handle their experiences as best they could.

---

*The names of all the children have been changed in order to protect their privacy.

THE CHILDREN

In September the children arrived at school with their parents, except for Mickey (5.0) and Peggy (4.9), who came on a bus with several older children who attended an educational class for children with special needs.

The children made what were to be their characteristic entries into the classroom. Timidly, almost reluctantly, Angela (4.7) entered noiselessly. Even at the end of the year she found it hard to separate from her mother. Wearing such a worried expression that it veiled the prettiness of her face, she was described (tongue-in-cheek) as an "ideal student" by Jean, who was concerned that she lacked verve and spontaneity. For much of the year she carefully skirted the adults in the room, actively selected and worked on materials, and only late in the year moved into cooperative activities.

Simon (4.5) was the largest boy in the group. At the end of the year 4'2", he towered by more than a foot above Brad (3.0), the youngest, smallest child in the group. Brad was not easily ignored when he decided to move into the room. He had a military bearing, walked with a ramrod-straight back, talked as briskly as he moved, and made his diminutive presence felt. Simon, in contrast, carried his tall, well-coordinated body apologetically. Jean described him as an "I wisher" because he frequently wished for things, most often food, in a wistful manner.

Peggy often was in the room before anyone realized, because she made a quiet, unobtrusive entrance. Early in November, Jean described Peggy in this way:

> Although slightly stout, Peggy carries her body firmly, erectly, and very carefully through space. Her eyes sparkle through her pink and polished face. Her friendly and warm smile is accompanied by inconsistent language. Her speech is slow, harsh, and severely delayed. Much of Peggy's language and actions are accomplished in a mechanical manner. She feels that the world around her needs to be careful and predictable. When it is, she smiles, and when it is not, she frowns painfully. Peggy's frequent and sometimes puzzling crying is rare now. Her preference for little bodily contact and her inability to verbalize her feelings make it a

perplexing task to understand and deal with Peggy's emotions. She works at being precise and perfect. Peggy is learning to predict, understand, and cope with a complex world. After many instances of running down a hill, tense and taut, clutching a teacher's hand, Peggy was able to solo! As she reluctantly moved down the hill she continually checked her side to reaffirm that the teacher was by her. Ever so quickly, Peggy lost control and toppled on her bottom. As she regained her awareness she looked up. Her scowl was quickly transformed into a beaming smile as she shouted in excitement to the world "*I f. . . . .llllll down,*" she pleased herself so.

And so to Robin (4.4) and Marcia (4.0), who were together in the school last year. They were firmly bonded in a relationship that had its smooth and stormy seasons. Jean described Robin:

Robin's round eyes and perfectly straight bangs accent his round cheeks, which take on an exaggerated shape as his lips articulate precisely each doctrine he espouses. His manner of play and interaction with others is systematic and dogmatic. Robin approaches life as a scientist looking for an answer. Once he has one, he incorporates it into his experience as fact. His life is full of many facts, and there is little if any tolerance for flexibility, dissonance, or "incorrectness." His encounters with experiences that may be challenging to his dogma are met with indignation. Robin reads fluently, and his comprehension (although again ruled by dogma) astounds all. He is very quick to inform other children, who read stories by retelling, that they are not really *reading*! And he is sure to approach a teacher with, "Kevin thinks he is reading, but I know he is not. He is not reading the words that are on the page!" Occasionally Robin's scholarly cap falls off as he gets entwined in the jubilant running, frolic, and laughter of his classmates.

Marcia will be discussed in detail later. For the time being, Jean has summed up the essence of this dynamo whose presence was felt the minute she stepped daintily and very cheerfully into the room: "Marcia is the builder with blocks, the conductor of trains, the belle of the ball, the artist at the easel, the poet, and the mother who takes care of and mothers all."

Johnny (3.1) was in school last year. Jean had seen his transformation from an aggressive angry 3, to a social 4-year-old. She wrote of him:

> Johnny's sparkling eyes and broad smile accent his friendly greetings. Over time he has made a great change in his approach to his peers. He is verbal, thoughtful, and sensitive. He has abandoned his "jump on their back and punch them in the stomach" approach. His play is constructive as he engages in a variety of activities. Recently he has taken great interest and pride in learning to read. An air of industriousness surrounds him as he writes word after word after word. A frequent question is "How do you spell _____?" We see Johnny as a whole person responding to his environment. One day, as he noticed and carefully observed Peggy crying and a teacher having little success at soothing her, Johnny approached. With Peggy's eyes gushing tears, Johnny leaned down, looked directly into Peggy's face, and with a look of puzzlement and empathy said, "Peggy, I don't know why you feel so sad, but sometimes it makes people feel a little more happy when someone does something for you. I'll make you a happy picture." As he turned he glanced at the teacher and said, "Maybe she'll feel better if I make her something happy." And he did! Johnny spends a lot of energy thinking and trying to understand. When puzzled and needing confirmation, he looks to adults. He wants to know the whos, whats, wheres, whens, and whys of his environment and actively pursues them through his play.

Unlike Johnny, Stuart (3.7) was new this year and had yet to find himself in a way that would permit him to become a more active and involved learner. He entered with a slightly bewildered look on his face. Jean said:

> Stuart is characterized by his propensity for music. He listens to and watches records and cassettes turn. He seems to hum along or feel the movement within. Its effect on him seems almost hypnotic. Stuart doesn't sing, which may be a result of his slow, limited, and usually garbled speech. When

not listening to music, Stuart spends most of his time playing with puzzles, plastic blocks, and small colored cubes. He
is systematic, careful, and usually lines blocks up, stacks,
sorts, or orders them in their boxes. His language seems to
make it difficult for him to communicate with his peers and
adults so he tends to spend most of his time by himself. Or
is it the reverse? that his solitary nature doesn't enable him
to practice language? Stuart is easygoing, cooperative, and
always willing to participate and help. Although sometimes
he seems to exist in a world of his own, when confronted by
his peers he usually responds to the situation.

Donald (3.5), unlike Stuart, took great pleasure in being in
a group of peers. He entered confidently, in charge of himself.
Jean said:

Donald's bouncy, bubbly nature and somewhat pudgy little
body are continually on the go! He retains his Australian accent and manner despite the forces of middle-class
Americanism. Donald is a determined little one. Sometimes
this makes him somewhat resistant to paying attention and
following rules. His independence is enriched by his many
skills and experiences. His confidence and determination are
not easily shattered—he will debate to the end with the best
of them. He enjoys being involved and where the action is.
Sometimes, with great enthusiasm, he wraps his arms
around a friend (male or female), and plants a kiss on the
person's cheek. Occasionally Donald will take on a mother-
hen nature. This usually occurs during times when children
are in a group. He will stretch his arms outward, look about
with disdain and scold "SHHH . . . SHHH . . . it's _____'s
turn!" But his childlike impulses and incessant conversation
usually make him the first violator of his own edict.

Another 3-year-old, Pat (3.1), initially cried a great deal at
separating from his mother but then settled down. Jean wrote:

Pat's oval face, pudgy cheeks, and fine wispy hair maintain
his babylike appearance. He seems to be growing faster than
he is ready. His language, emotions, and interactions are

portrayed in a confident, definitive, and serious manner. His thought conveys that he is a 3-year-old: "This is so because it's like that. Just because it is. Because I said so." These are his reasons. He is governed by his observations. He enjoys playing with others and usually participates in a variety of activities. Pat does have his favorites. He likes cars and blocks. He will continually reconfirm as he goes about show-ing everyone, "This is my car. It's orange. It's the Dukes' car. See, it's orange. It rolls fast, too." Pat usually seems happy and content, handles mishaps with a stiff upper lip, and real ly *likes* to play.

The twin girls were identical, except that Lee (3.4) was slightly larger than Lynne (3.4). Their pretty faces, light giggly voices, and similar ways of approaching persons and objects had made it hard to distinguish between them. These merry little girls enjoyed the confusion and teased everyone. Their morning en-try was a hide-and-seek game when they loved to surprise every-one by appearing and then vanishing into the hall. It was char-acteristic of both girls to observe carefully before they acted. Jean said, "Slowly, ever so slowly, they approach and finally over time engage [in an activity]." They were aesthetically alive; they en-gaged in much dramatic play, and both girls enjoyed sitting on an adult's lap to hear stories, which absorbed them.

So at the beginning of the year there were Robin, Marcia, and Simon ready to be social; shy, reserved Stuart retreating to the tape box day after day; Johnny with a new interest in aca-demics that seemed to be a sublimation of his former aggressive attacks on children; Brad, who entered every day to take up a watchful guarded position in his cubby; the twin girls, who ten-tatively joined the group for a few minutes, then darted away to hide; Donald, Angela, Pat, and Brad, who, as is common at their age, played parallel a great deal; Angela and Peggy, both of whom cried a great deal early in the year; and Kevin (3.0), who entered the group late, an imaginative, lively boy who belonged at once.

Robin, Marcia, and Simon, having spent the previous year with Jean, were the knowing, influential old-timers. Mickey and Peggy found each other rapidly every day, perhaps bonded together by the experience they shared on the minibus and the half day in the behavior modification clinic. Their presence in the nursery school with Jean was on a trial basis. Mickey, who will be described more fully later, darted around the room, eyes fixed on one of the adults. Peggy, pink and plump, remained fixed, talked very little, and moved away from the water table for group meetings only reluctantly. It was hard to understand the few words Mickey and Peggy spoke.

These were the children Jeff found himself teaching as acting lead teacher in the fall with Jean floating in and out of the room, always observing, frequently coteaching. Although he had been placed with Jean as an undergraduate psychology major the previous spring, being in charge of the class was a new and challenging experience.

BELIEFS EMERGE

Every day Jean and Jeff talked over the session. Once a week these conversations were tape-recorded, transcribed, and later read in order to infer underlying values and beliefs about children, teaching, and education.

Jean expressed a belief that the children brought a wealth of knowledge to school with them. They began acquiring this wealth from infancy on, sorting, grouping, classifying, and generalizing about the events, persons, and things they encountered. This knowledge she viewed as the outcome of their active search to make sense out of their lives and to know themselves more deeply. Some of this knowledge would remain uniquely personal to them which she wanted to validate, but she also wanted to connect and expand the children's experiences with knowledge derived from the disciplines such as geography, literature, and mathematics.

She felt, too, that it was possible for children to achieve these objectives because of their incessant search for meaning. Some of their behavior mystified her by not following the laws of adult logic, but she believed that, like adults, they had their reasons.

Children's Reasons

Evidence of this set of values and beliefs emerged very early in the fall conversations as Jeff plunged into the maelstrom of acting as lead teacher. His first morning was far from smooth; in his words, "It all went crazy."

JEAN: What made you think it was crazy today?

JEFF: I looked around the room and it seemed like . . . every time I turned around something else was happening and I didn't know what was going on.

JEAN: What kind of things were happening?

JEFF: Um, when it first dawned on me is when I started to work with one child, and you said, "Someone's—Emma's* putting water on . . . "

JEAN: Emma was pumping water on Brad.

JEFF: Right, and you said, "I'll let you handle it," and I said, "Oops—*I* have to do all this now." [laughs] I had to be aware of all these things happening. And after that it just seemed like one thing after another, you know, everything seemed to be going . . . more haywire than I remember it. Even that . . . apple-cutting-up session. Everything just didn't run as smoothly . . . I didn't know if I was just totally not running things right, or if the kids are different than the ones I was used to, or . . .

In her first question about what made him think it was crazy, Jean reflects her belief in human beings of all ages as gatherers of evidence out of which to spin meaning. She steers Jeff in the direction of observing events, so that he can stand back and re-evaluate "crazy." Jeff has been disconcerted by the activities he saw as frantic and disconnected, children "climbing the wall" so to speak.

JEFF: It did seem like there were kids all over the place. Not the group of kids that I remember from last semester; there would

---

*Emma was moved to another group early in the semester.

be a group at the blocks, a group at the water table, one at the clay, and that was about it.

JEAN: Yeah.

JEFF: . . . or some as the dress-up area, . . . but they clumped.

In her response, Jean expressed her view of the essential rationality, purposefulness, and meaningful intentions of young children.

JEAN: The group that you worked with last time, again, it was the second semester so they had already gotten used to each other, and they were a bit older, and used to interacting together more. Also some of the children are young. It's the beginning of the year, they don't have those experiences, and for a long time it's not going to be very pleasant for them to be interacting, because if they're used to being at home and having lots of undivided attention, that's what they're used to—so when you sit down with them they're expecting that. They're expecting to be able to use the blocks all by themselves. So if someone comes over and takes the blocks away from them or starts to share the blocks, or wants to use the blocks with them, it might not be very pleasant for them at first, because they are used to having undivided everything: materials, attention.

Jean helped Jeff think about how the world seemed to them, reflecting on the feelings they might have been experiencing. Jeff recalled the overwhelming rush to help him cut the apples for snack time. He had not anticipated everyone wanting to cut the fruit, and he felt bewildered as the children struggled to handle the knives. Jean searched as a detective would to find clues that would unlock the meaning to him of the children's behavior. She went back to the children's development and pointed out this might well be the first time for many that they had been allowed to handle a knife—an exciting experience for them! She suggested in the future putting out the apples before cutting them so that the children could wonder why they were there, preparing them for what was to come so they could think reflectively. She also provided the rationality of the rush to Jeff. She does not see small children as irrational, empty-headed seekers of stimuli. They have their purposes and interests.

As the conversation continued, she singled out the rush to the table to make sense of it from the viewpoint of the children. Jean recalled:

> As I looked around the room, it was Marcia who seemed to be directing a lot of the activity, or directing the flow of the day, for at least two or three other children. And then there was Emma, who was leading Brad around. The first day Emma told Brad everything that he should do, really took him under her wing . . . now he's starting to branch off a little more by himself, but she still has gone over to him and said "Come on, it's time to do this now. . . ."
>
> So you were at the table with apples and Marcia wanted to go cut the apples, then Marcia came with two children that she was carrying around with her, and with Emma came Brad, and Emma might have wanted to cut apples, but Brad might not have wanted to. And Marcia might have wanted to cut apples, but the other two children might not want to, and I think as time goes on, as children, um . . . maybe in a few months if Marcia and Angela are playing and Marcia says, "Come on, let's go cut apples," Angela might say, "No, I don't want to." But a possibility now is that she followed Marcia over. So that you're getting children for lots of different reasons.

Children's reasons recur as a theme Jean pursued with Jeff in a variety of contexts.

A number of teachers would have spent this first conference inducting Jeff into their belief that the beginning of the school year is the time to set rules and regulations, other events being secondary to this. Jean valued harmonious group living with its necessary rules, but they were not her first priority. She believed they ought to be the outcome of understanding children and designing appropriate educational activities. Her first aim was to see the world through the children's eyes. Techniques for managing classroom life served the understandings generated by this perspective.

In her conversations with Jeff about Marcia early in the academic year, she put into practice her belief about viewing situations from the child's view. In these conversations, Marcia's usage of power as a leader frequently surfaced as a concern for Jeff because he felt she did not give other children breathing space. We all noticed that on those rare occasions when Marcia did not attend school, a sense of someone missing, a certain stillness, marked the day; her presence and her influence were food for thought. Jeff initially searched for management techniques to reduce her overactive leadership in order to give the other children a chance.

In the following conversation, Jeff thought about techniques he could provide that would stop Marcia from "beating the other kids to the punch" during group meetings. He wondered about going around the circle, giving each person a chance to talk. Jean had reservations about procedures and techniques becoming ritualistic and mechanical, so she refocused the discussion on the significance and meaning of leadership to Marcia.

In responding to Jeff, Jean recalled what she knew about Marcia both within and outside of school. She tried to reconstruct Marcia's world in a way that would account for her overly energetic leadership. She tried to gain a fuller understanding of this small girl before moving in with strategies to guide her in ways that could be beneficial for all.

Marcia had grown up with her mother and maternal grandparents. Three loving adults had provided an admiration circle for this delightful girl who was used to having her ideas applauded and relished. There was always a listening ear and a willing playmate. Her sense of autonomy and initiative had flowered and with it her confidence and abilities.

The minute she found herself in a nursery group, she was thoroughly at home, and in no time she was taking charge when occasion arose. And Jean recalled, with some chagrin, that last year she had sometimes provided those occasions. She told Jeff, "it got to the point where lots of times I had questions, I'd want to pose them, and I'd find myself looking toward the children who were more verbal—like Marcia—and not necessarily giving the others a chance." She encouraged Jeff to make observations over time on Marcia's leadership, not interpreting his records through his or Marcia's eyes but putting himself in the children's places. (Marcia's leadership is discussed in more detail in Chapter 5, and some of its meanings for the children are examined.)

Jean helped Jeff move away from focusing on the right technique to manage Marcia, directing him toward first understanding the dynamics that influenced this child. Given this understanding, the need for teaching Marcia remained.

Children's Needs

Jean saw a compelling need for Marcia to learn to listen to other children and adults and to receive guidance in doing this in the group: "helping Marcia gain some control so that when she moves into a free play situation with other children and another child starts to talk, she might stop and listen. Hopefully, from the group situation, it might transfer to another time."

Jean viewed children as needing help in order to make educated sense of their world, part of which involves helping them work together, so that they can both learn from and teach each other. She told Jeff:

> It's important for you to be there with them as they're start-
> ing to form those groups—and incorporating more people,
> so that you're not sitting there block-building with one child,
> but incorporating other children so you can work through
> the process with them, of developing the necessary skills
> that they would use in cooperative play. I don't think it's
> something that happens . . . um, naturally . . . I think it isn't
> something that happens by itself.

Jean conveyed the same message to Sue, an assistant teacher, who, late in February, noted on her weekly 3″ × 5″ cards on the children:

> It sure was noisy today. Stuart was great. This is the first
> time I've seen him do something besides puzzles and blocks.
> He spent a lot of time at the water table and really seemed
> to enjoy it. He was playing more in groups, too. It was really
> nice to see that.

Jean responded, "Did you notice anyone in particular that he interacted well with, so another time you might try to initiate some activity between them?"

From her encouraging Sue to observe children's initiatives and move in to support them one can infer Jean's belief that children are not wildflowers that grow without human intervention. They are part of the human family, and they need human support and teaching. For this support and teaching they do not come empty-handed or empty-headed. They come fully equipped to engage actively in learning.

Children's Capacities

Jean viewed children as learners who have impressive capacities of mind that are complex and not fully charted. In this belief she was supported by a growing body of psychological research, including the studies on infant development. But this view is not universally held by the public and professionals, including those in the field of education.

In a recent publication of the Association for Supervision and Curriculum Development, one educator presented a widely held view when he wrote, "Young children lack fundamental knowledge, lack basic skills and processes for self-learning and require learning activities that place them in relatively passive roles as learners" (Valverde, 1982, p. 83). In light of this belief, the invasion of kindergartens by prepackaged worksheet programs, filled by still, silent listening children is understandable.

In another highly influential publication, a view of children's young minds is presented that leads one to conclude they are ready for acquisition of basic skills but lack the complexity to reach the deeper goals possible for secondary school children. The authors point out that they chose elementary schools to study because the educational goals there are clear, stating, "there is fairly general agreement that the fundamental tool skills of language, arts and mathematics form the heart of the early elementary" (Brophy & Evertson, 1979, p. 152). They continue by indicating the complexity of curricula at the high school level and ask, "For example, which of the following should be the primary goal of a high school teacher: reading comprehension, writing and composition skills, expressing thoughts with creativity and originality, being able to apply what one reads to one's personal life?" (p. 153). From Jean's perspective, except for writing and composition skills, the same goals apply in early childhood education. Young children who read *Goodnight Moon* until it was dog-eared let her know that they were searching for ways to cope with the difficult feelings they experienced at separating from those they loved. They showed that they could and did apply what they read to their personal lives. The poems, stories, and word construction of young children attested to their "creativity and originality," their capacity to be the linguistic geniuses of Chukofsky's vision (1971).

Jean's beliefs about children were set in bold relief by the general responses of many of the psychology undergraduates when they first entered the classroom. Enthusiastic, interested, able young people, they were often headed toward medical school, graduate psychology, or related human service professions. Idealistic for the most part, they did not want to be dehumanized, remote functionaries but looked forward to building warm relationships as part of their work life. They liked their placements in the nursery school, stayed after the sessions to chat, and revisited when the semester officially ended.

Although matters changed by the end of the semester, most of the students initially tended to fall into a consistent pattern. They talked rather loudly to all the children at once, often insisting on eye contact, and they laughed together at the "cute" things the children did or said. The children seemed to be objects in need of reinforcement, a word that was much favored. In common with many professionals and students in other disciplines as well as education, they had learned to think of children in terms of norms and of their interactions with them as standardized events calling for the application of reliable techniques. When reality did not neatly match their theoretical formulations, these thoughtful young people waged intellectual battles with each other and Jean. Bud and Jeff worked together as undergraduate assistant teachers in the spring and had known Johnny as an acting-out fury at that time. They were pleasantly surprised at his transformation in the fall semester and tried to account for it. Jeff discussed this with Jean:

JEFF: I was mentioning to Bud today that Johnny was a lot different now from last year . . . and we were saying how it's hard to reinforce some things. How can you say something like, "Thank you, Johnny, for not knocking anyone's head off today"?

    JEAN: What *could* you say?

    JEFF: Well, I don't know. . . . There are times when he might say "excuse me" to someone. Then we'd reinforce that—"Johnny, I'm glad to see . . . " or if he waits for someone in line, waits for someone to move.

Motivation

A belief in the teacher as reinforcer, as the dispenser of praise, conditioning goodness or badness in children, has been very widely held for centuries and currently this view finds support in Skinnerian theory. Changes in children are explained away in terms of teacher interventions. The problem is that the explanation applied to Johnny and others does not let the teacher enter into the complexities of Johnny's inner life. His improved behavior may have been the outcome of conscious experimentation, undertaken probably with home and teacher guidance. Jean believed children did attempt civilized ways of interacting with others freely of their own choosing. She saw children in need of support in doing this, not reinforcement that excludes them from the dynamics of the process. In observations of her classroom, she made a few reinforcing comments such as, "That's great!" or "I like that," but many comments of support: "You found a wide space for the box" (on the wide box sculpture), or, "Thanks for passing the peanuts, Mickey. Stuart needs some." She gave the children the bases for her appreciation or judgment.

Her concern about conditioning children was illustrated in this conversation with Jeff. As a new teacher, he was rightly concerned with effecting smooth transitions. In one conversation, he reflected about the previous day when, following a group meeting, the children had rushed wildly to the three tables with material set up on them.

    JEAN: You just wanted to get them to the table [laughter], "And they're off!" [more laughter]. Sometimes I get concerned about that, when they know group time is coming to an end and they're "on the gates"—so I've been trying to vary that sometimes. . . .

JEFF: Yeah . . . yeah.

JEAN: Just so it doesn't become so routine—I mean, once they get there they usually become very involved in the materials that are there, but sometimes it's like . . . a pigeon in a box—so routine. So I try to make it so that what gets them there isn't routine, but interest, rather than, um . . . a conditioned response. . . .

JEFF: I used that, of course; get them motivated and show them something neat, and then: "Let's go!" [laughter]. Maybe I encouraged that a little too much.

Jeff jokingly presented a widely held view that children need external motivation by a teacher or by materials in order to learn. Jeff expressed this view initially when he pondered with Jean about the children's fascination with Play-Doh and water:

> It seems like, if kids are that interested and they do a
> lot of different things [with water and Play-Doh] that they
> ought to be learning a lot of things there. At the water table
> where they're pouring—pour, pour, pour. . . . It's hard to get
> a handle on what it is that's so motivating in that . . . the
> attributes of water? Maybe it's the same with Play-Doh.

Autonomy and Initiative

Teachers who hold to a view of themselves or materials as the motivators teach out of a set of beliefs that legitimizes their exercise of power at the expense of children's initiative. Jean believed healthy children were intrinsically motivated, and this belief led her to trust them as learners active on their own behalf. She believed that she must protect their sense of autonomy, their sense of their own competency, and that there must be room in the day for their exertion of initiative in carrying out purposes they felt deeply. She drew on Erikson's stage formulation of psychosocial development in defining what she meant by healthy growth and development, which called for feelings of trust, a sense of autonomy, and thrusts of initiative in the children.

Through their use of materials and an allocation of time, she believed that children revealed and expanded much of their thinking, provided that their developmental needs for autonomy and initiative were respected. Marcia held many interesting ideas and chatted freely about them, but when adult demands were imposed, she became restricted. A student teacher for a project asked Marcia to draw a picture for her, which she completed in very short order:

> MARCIA: I'm making feet now. I forgot eyes. There! I'm done.
>
> S.TEACHER: What is it?
>
> SIMON: It's a duck.
>
> S.TEACHER: Tell me about your duck.
>
> MARCIA: [in tones of scorn and disbelief at such a request] I *just* made him! [laughs]
>
> SIMON: Quack. Quack.
>
> MARCIA: He goes quack quack. There! We're all done.

It was as if Marcia said to herself, "These adults! What next? I may as well get this piece of nonsense over and done with so I can get on with my real work." Teacher-imposed tasks did not always release the same energy for problem solving and imaginative work as those that Marcia undertook of her own volition.

The children did work hard, sometimes at tasks set for them. But Jean observed children working hard and long at problem-solving tasks they set for themselves, calling for concentration. She saw them pursuing their ends when it called for efforts devoid of fun; building and rebuilding, frustrated that a ramp was not right or an enclosure had no effective gate; converging on the large cardboard box group sculpture in small group discussions about where the newly painted item might fit best, making reference to its color, shape, size, and relationship to other objects. She saw them as human learners intent on becoming competent, testing their ideas, experiencing some confusion, some perplexity, and occasionally some enlightenment. She recognized the intellectual bridges Simon had yet to cross when, on his fifth birthday, he told 4-year-old Marcia, "*Now* I'm older than you are," but she appreciated that age relationships were on his mind. Simon took his own initiative in building a concept of time, and so did the other children. Jean tried to incorporate this personal knowledge when she taught ideas about time in less personal terms as part of the education program.

From Jean's viewpoint, autonomy and initiative had to be experienced by children under guidance because they needed practice in making decisions. She did value their healthy development as persons, but her view was also fixed on the distant years when they would be voting citizens in the democracy. She believed that the foundations for beginning to behave wisely as a participant in society were laid down in early childhood. She viewed the children as competent to engage in decision making, able to resolve many small dilemmas and conflicts themselves. Generally, she rejected playing the role of referee for many reasons discussed later. Marcia and Robin, close at times, often had minor spats. Jean tried not to get caught in the middle of these conflicts.

One morning at the painting table Marcia snatched up a piece of paper Robin had taken for himself but left unguarded for a few minutes. Brad was a witness to this. Robin complained to Jean in a whiny tone, and Jean dipped into this conflict briefly with one question to him: "Did you show her where the paper was?" His whiny tone evaporated as he acknowledged in a lower tone that he had not. Jean left the two 4-year-old antagonists with young Brad at the paint table.

Jean chose not to act as a referee between Robin and Marcia, but she pointed the way to one solution and left. There was a mesh of ideas and feelings behind her response. Robin's occasional whininess can be wearing to her; she remembered that he had been sick and grouchy the day before, but she trusted his strength and his ability to solve this small but intensely felt problem in his way. So her few words came from a foundation of beliefs, understandings, and feelings, recognizing her own limits and yet entering the world of Robin so she could feel for him even though he irritated her from time to time.

Children's Feelings

Jean viewed children as having the complex, deep feelings that are part of the human condition. Those who hold views of young children as less complex than youth and adults continue to deny that children have these feelings. It is only in recent decades, and certainly not universally, that the anguish and pain young children in hospitals suffer are finding recognition (Beuf,

1979). Observing young children who spend long days in day care, one is impressed by their coping power but also reminded that, necessary as day care is, it is often a difficult experience for them. (This is not a negative vote for day care but a strong plea to recognize that it is not easy for many young children and that their feelings must be acknowledged.) Even in his short sessions, young Brad spent time missing his mother. Denying that he had such feelings would have distanced Jean and the other adults from his world, thus preventing them from helping him work through his feelings in order to be free for the rich compensatory encounters of group living. Several of the children had fathers whose work took them away for days, sometimes weeks. On many occasions, Jean initiated discussion, for example, of how Simon had felt when he missed his father and how sad Brad was when his father had to be away two weeks. The children involved were given a chance to acknowledge their distress.

Jean recognized children as having strong feelings because they are human beings. This recognition extended to everyone in the room. The assistant teacher and student teachers expressed their negative and positive feelings freely in conversations and on the 3″ × 5″ cards they wrote to Jean regularly. On one such card, Sue wrote, "Boy was Peggy *great* today! She talked at group meeting, and all through the day. It really makes me excited to see her talking and getting involved with the other children." Jean replied with an emphatic "*Yes!*"

On another day, Sue wrote on her card, "We went for a walk outside and Mickey slipped on the ice. He was crying, and Peggy went over to him and took his hand and walked with him 'til he stopped crying." Jean wrote back, "Who says kids are self-centered?" Unfortunately, Piaget's concept of egocentrism in early childhood continues to be misinterpreted in some quarters as self-centeredness or selfishness.

It seems likely that Jean's awareness of the complex feelings of children accounted partially for the compassion and caring that young Brad, Marcia, and the other children showed to Mickey, to new adults who entered the room, and to young visitors. They could be sure that their own distresses and their own joys would register with Jean. The children knew this, but occasionally a parent would misread her quiet, contained manner.

One day, rather depressed by a parent who criticized her for being low-key with the children, she summed up part of her belief about the nature of her work as a teacher, and the message she gave children: "Everything isn't going to be wonderful and exciting. I'm not a clown to promise them wonderful things as if they are at a carnival." School was a workplace where human beings gathered together, ultimately becoming a cohesive group with all the potential that healthy groups possess for moving persons forward toward fuller human lives. Her classroom was a workshop—not a Romper Room or a Ding-Dong School. The classroom climate was positive. Visitors felt it. (Collecting teacher utterances and using Withall's instrument (1967) on them supported this assertion quantitatively.) But beneath the surface there were conflicting pulls, and Jean had to live with these and the pressures they exerted on her.

The students brought various conflicts to the classroom. Initially, some expressed either subtle anger or open discontent that she offered them no "script." They tended, at least part of the time, to see children as trainable objects, worrying about "reinforcing them inappropriately" and occasionally chastising Jean for so doing. Despite these undercurrents, as the weeks passed, most of them showed a genuine caring and interest in children, added to the warmth of the classroom, and designed original and often stimulating materials. Jean encouraged open discussion and was nonpunitive of views she found anathema, accepting these learners as they were, as she did child learners. It made for an alive group of children and adults, periodically pausing in uncertainty, then moving with energy to a new place, fueled by the educational program described in a later chapter. It is time now to move on to look specifically at some of Jean's beliefs about herself as a teacher, and at some events that flowed from these.

3 Jean's Perspectives on Teaching

Jean's perspectives on children and her beliefs about education gave direction and depth to what she believed she should do as a teacher. Seeing herself as the children's ally in their search for unique private as well as shared public meanings, she was faced with balancing how much freedom to give them to make their own way and how much she should direct. Sharing teacher power with young, inexperienced groups of children is not a smooth process, and in the climate of contemporary schooling, there is evidence that it is becoming more the exception than the rule. Many classrooms revolve around the teacher, dominated by teacher talk. Hyman (1980) points out that in recent studies of classroom talk, a very small percentage was made up of children's questions. McNeil (1982) notes that we have arrived at a stage when teacher dominance is the mode. Reflecting on earlier studies of laissez-faire, democratic, and autocratic teaching, he points out that "unlike the teaching model of the 1950's, the 'good' teacher is neither laissez-faire nor democratic but controlling. The teacher controls the instructional goals, chooses materials appropriate for the student's ability, and paces the instructional sequence" (pp. 27–28). While these educators draw their conclusions from studies in school settings for older children, teacher-controlled programs are evident in many kindergartens, day care centers, and nursery schools.

SHARING DECISION MAKING

Jean swam against a growing tide in creating an environment where children were permitted to make many decisions, shored up by her beliefs about their needs for autonomy and initiative and their capacities to put them to good use.

Jean believed teachers ought to allow children the time to

solve problems in their own imprecise way. In one conference she cautioned Jeff against being the referee:

JEFF: One thing I said to Margaret the other day was, one of my big problems is getting into the role of referee . . . when children fight over a truck or something. And I was saying how I don't like to get into that sort of thing because . . . it calls for quick action, maybe, and it's hard to think of the right thing to say, and . . . you could say something wrong and it's bad, and maybe they could have worked it out for themselves. All these different little problems! What about a general principle to avoid implying things you don't want to when you say something?

JEAN: I think part of the problem of not feeling you're a referee is not setting yourself up as a referee. Giving the kids some opportunity to solve their own problems—not intervening right away. Approaching them maybe, and sitting there, and going through a process that develops very slowly . . . "Well, see what do *you* think might be a solution?" so that they see themselves as solving the problem. So then you don't set yourself up as the one who always jumps in and solves the problem, and who makes all the decisions. So when I send all of them over to you to find out if we're going outside . . .

JEFF: Then I can say, "What do you think? . . . "

JEAN: Yeah, so they can see themselves as making some of the decisions.

Her belief that children needed to experience some autonomy and express their initiative found its counterpart in her beliefs about what she as a teacher should do. In practice, this meant that Jean often did not act. As an observer, on a few occasions when children were in conflict, I was impressed by Jean's ability to refuse to intervene and simply to observe, with understanding and faith, how the children tackled their problem. From my armchair, it was tempting to impose an efficient adult solution on a problem, but Jean had the strength to live with the uncertainty generated by the decision making of children. In the following incident in which children took charge, Jean saw some positive results.

A problem arose over sharing a particularly desirable pair of scissors. Early in the year, the group had developed a norm about sharing, and Brad violated that norm when he refused to give the scissors to Marcia, who was outraged:

MARCIA: Brad won't share. He won't share his scissors. I just needed it for a minute.

JEAN: Maybe he still needs it. There are plenty of scissors.

BRAD: [looking cross] No one can use the bigger one—that's mine. [Perhaps this is a special pair of scissors?]

MARCIA
AND PAT: [whispering in Brad's ear] I don't like you. I won't play with you 'cause you won't share.

[Jean has walked away.]

MARCIA: I'm telling Sue. [She tells Sue, the psychology student, who, having observed Jean, reacts noncommittally.]

PAT: Donald's gonna give me his scissors, and we'll both have scissors.

MARCIA: [who has gone to get scissors] I'll give you mine, Pat.

[Brad goes on painting and holding on to the scissors.]

MARCIA: [very haughtily] I don't like you. You don't share.

This was too much for Brad, who told her contritely, "I'll share my stuff," and was forgiven. Marcia had learned that direct appeals work, that children are not beholden to adults for ready-made solutions. Perhaps the power of human relationships and the impact of negotiation had touched her. Certainly, whatever self-centered world engaged Brad, the threat of being excluded from Marcia's circle reminded him that he was one of a group, not the center of the universe. Had Jean voiced and enforced the rule, "We must share," this small learning experience would have been displaced by a routine ritual, representing an unexamined introjection of adult values and authority.

Susan Isaacs (1930) in the Malting House School made a pioneering effort to see where the strength of children's intelligence could take them. She believed they needed to face the consequences of their actions. This sometimes led to uneven times when the children went off to play and "forgot" to wash their luncheon or supper dishes, so that the next time they needed them there was an unpleasant washing-up job to be done. In the era when some early childhood classrooms have the sterile neatness of hospital rooms, it is worth reflecting on the notion that important learning cannot be achieved without some disarray, some unevenness, some uncertainty, even some mistakes.

Sources of Discovery

There were some times when Jean intervened and used her authority directly. But these were times she had to justify to herself as being consonant with her objective to help the children become more competent in the area of decision making. In the following conversation, she mused ruefully about an episode that took place early in the year. It had not been a very good morning: Marcia's voice had rung dominantly, bossing everyone within hearing range, Robin had humorlessly laid down and enforced his latest regulations, and Simon had moped around most unassertively. In Jean's words:

> Well, today there was one instance where Robin found a lotto game on the shelf. And he just took to that (I think we talked about Robin and his rules and his games), and he carefully set the cards out on the floor and put all the others by the box, and he went and brought certain children over, Peggy and Stuart, and had them sit by their cards and explained how it was going to be his turn first, and then this one, and went through all of the rules, and he was very careful, or seemed to be very careful, about the children he chose. And along comes Marcia, and she didn't like the rules, right away, off the bat, because Robin was going first, so Marcia left, and then Simon came over, and then Marcia decided that she wanted to play after all. So she just banished Simon and said: "Get up, I'm playing there, it's my turn," and Simon got up and left. And . . . I don't know at what point I picked up on it—I think it was when Simon went over sulking to his cubby, and I asked him what happened, and he said, "I was playing, and she came and took my card away, and said that she was playing." I asked him if he still wanted to play and he said "yes," so I went over and told Marcia that Simon still wanted to play, and, in that instance, even though I try and encourage the children to do

the talking—for some reason I decided to tell Marcia that Simon was playing there, and that she'd have to wait until later, and that she'd . . . have to find something else to do.

Then it just got really confused, and that's when I find that I do best when I don't interfere with the children's interactions. Then Marcia got up, and she looked at Simon and she said, "Do you want to play, Simon?" And he said, "Well, no, I don't want to play anymore." So I felt like I went through this whole thing, and was really a bit harsh on Marcia, and then when she finally got up and left, Simon didn't want to play anymore; Robin was aggravated with me that the game was disrupted when it was his turn, the two other children who had been there left the scene, didn't want to play anymore, so I really—um.

MARGARET: You blew it! [laughs].

JEAN: I messed up the whole thing—they could have been doing wonderful things—matching pictures! [laughter]

One of the hallmarks of Jean's professional practice was her continual analysis and assessment of her work to ensure consistency with her educational beliefs and intentions. In this engagement with the children, she felt, she had made a mistake. She did not have to expend energy proving herself right under all conditions. The inevitability of making mistakes in this laboratory of human interactions was acknowledged and accepted as a small price to pay for the substantial increments of active learning in which all engaged. In his discussion of professional practice, Schön (1983) says that mistakes, and the ensuing "uncertainty, can become a source of discovery rather than an occasion for self-defense" (p. 299).

Jean permitted the children to experiment at finding their own solutions to problems because she believed in the group's wisdom in concert with guidance she provided. She was committed to experiments and consequently to some failures in decision making.

Many adults in society seem uncomfortable with the buzz of classrooms full of active children. Fox Butterfield's (1981) comments in the *New York Times* were echoed by many Americans who visited China. He said:

> American visitors to China are continually impressed, indeed often amazed, by the almost universal good behavior of Chinese children. They are quiet, obedient, quick to follow their teachers' instructions, and they seldom exhibit the boisterous aggressiveness or selfishness of American children.

"Being quiet, obedient, and quick to follow their teachers' instructions" are qualities that match later expectations in a society where one is told what to do and where to do it. In the USSR I observed a group of children in a docile, cheerful way play at "manicurist" with real nail polish and direct instructions from the teacher-director of the play. There was nothing boisterous about this, but the level of initiative and decision making was very low.

However, the charge that North American children are selfish is grave, and Jean did reflect on the balance between children's needs as individuals and as group members. Much in our society directs us toward competitiveness for self-aggrandizement and induces egocentrism. Bombarded as our young children are by media messages glorifying personal acquisition of products, which is equated with self-worth, the processes of group living, such as sharing and turn taking, are made additionally difficult for them. But no matter where they live, children in groups have to share, and Jean believed there was value in this, her objective being to have the children self-regulate behaviors that would enable them to learn from and through each other.

BALANCING INDIVIDUAL AND GROUP NEEDS

Early childhood teachers and parents of young children know how difficult it is to learn to share, so one of the objectives of preschool is to help children do this out of the practical knowledge of their developing experience. Jean believed that materials should be shared, but she steered away from arbitrary, adult-imposed rules about this. As she said:

> I feel that just because children are in the room doesn't necessarily mean that they need to share all of the materials

all of the time. Sometimes it's good for them to have the feeling that . . . sometimes you have materials to yourself; work by yourself. I've seen instances where teachers will say . . . "Today is Monday, and so it's A, B, and C's day to play with the blocks." And just children A, B, and C can play with the blocks. On Wednesday, D, E, and F will play with the blocks.

The Logic of the Play

Jeff speculated that it could be "unfair" when a child monopolized all the blocks or other materials and accessories. Jean agreed that it could be, but, before making a decision to intervene, she always tried to consider the logic of the play. Consistent with her beliefs, she asks, What do these materials mean now to this child? If Simon has been working all morning on a three-stall garage and has commandeered the only three buses, should he be made to share one of them with Marcia, who decides she wants one? Jean thought about what boundaries are set and when in terms of one child's freedom to pursue solitary interests in a group setting. To resolve this, Jean had to call upon her observations and recordings of the children. Mindlessly voicing a "we-must-share" rule might solve the conflict superficially, but it is not helpful if Simon's need was to learn how to hold on to what he had, or if Marcia's need was to recognize the complexities of others' worlds and their satisfaction in taking an initiative and seeing it through to fruition.

Jean could live with a child's playing alone, temporarily holding on to materials that normally would be shared, because of her belief in the social drives that propel children into group work. She told Jeff:

> I think that's part of the *built-in beauty* of encouraging lots of socialization between the children. You have a situation in which every day Robin doesn't go in and build his own building, but there's Robin and maybe three or four other children who are working on the building together; there's a kind of a community spirit.

This community spirit was actively supported by Jean, who worked assiduously throughout the day helping the children make connections with each other. One day Angela's father had left on a trip, and she was weeping sadly. Brad was watching her looking very forlorn.

> SIMON: My dad went on a trip and I missed him, too.
> JEAN: Remember your dad went on a trip, Brad? You went to the airport.
> BRAD: He went to Kansas.

Brad had been very upset by his father's week-long absence, but he now reflected on it cheerfully. Jean had spun the empathic thread that connected the separation experiences of the three young children, a step in forging a community spirit of mutual caring, which is basic to effective participation in the group or community of the classroom.

Living with Unevenness

The children were working hard at learning how to function as a group. At the end of May they had made considerable headway, but the process was uneven. It was hard for them to take turns, to balance assertion of their individual rights with responsible commitment to those of others in the group. Intent on their own need to be next, the children had a hard time keeping in mind the just ordering of events, as illustrated in the following episode.

Some of the children wanted to be traced in order to make silhouettes of their bodies and, slowly and unevenly, they worked out a way of proceeding. Stuart, Donald, Johnny, Simon, Pat, and Angela watched. Jean was momentarily busy in another part of the room.

> SIMON: I'm the first one's gonna do it.
> CHORUS: I'm next.
> DONALD: I'm after Stuart.
> ANGELA: I'm after Simon.
> JOHNNY: You know what? I'll be next.
> ANGELA: How about that—Stuart, then you, then Simon?

CHORUS: Me next!

DONALD: I asked first.

CHORUS: I asked first.

JOHNNY: I'll be next. No! I am. No! I am.

[At this stage Jean joins the group.]

SIMON: [virtuously, as Jean traces Johnny] It's really my turn. [Donald goes next, lying down on the paper. Jean asks Johnny to trace him.]

SIMON: After Donald it's my turn.

[Johnny is holding a blue crayon.]

SIMON: Johnny, you got the color I want . . . so . . . so . . . That's for me, right?

JOHNNY: [very pleased] Simon wants me to trace him, because I've got the color he wants me to trace him.

And so everyone was traced, not strictly in turn, but with an opportunity to negotiate and to cooperate. Some assertion was shown by Simon, who made an agreement with Johnny that satisfied both boys, and aloof Angela moved in with a constructive suggestion. She bore no grudge that it was not taken.

Jean recognized the complex demands that sharing and taking turns made on young children, but she believed in their capacities to deal with the complexity of being a person and being a group member. We talked together about their responsiveness to two stories with quite different messages. They had sat very still and very silent at the respective times they heard the stories, and phrases from them hung in the air as the children later talked and laughed about their content. Both stories about vegetables, *The Carrot Seed* and the folktale *The Turnip*, they record in one instance the triumph of the person alone against the world and in the other the victory that comes only from being a group member. In the relatively contemporary story *The Carrot Seed*, a small boy plants a seed and holds to his faith that it will grow despite the doubts of his big brother, his mother, and his father. In the old folktale *The Turnip*, a child goes out to the field to pull up a turnip, fails to do it, and fails again and again as various family members come to join the growing chain. It is only when all the family pulls together that the enormous turnip emerges.

The children acted out these stories with great energy, providing a reflection of the stories' meaning for them and dynamic evidence of their abilities to see the many sides of reality. Jean believed teachers could and should help them grow in these abilities.

FACILITATING ALL AS TEACHER-LEARNERS

Jean believed that participation as group members developed the children more fully as persons. Far from sacrificing their individuality, she thought, the children became more trusting and more autonomous, and they showed more initiative through their participation as members in the small community. In her work as a teacher she wanted to enable children to learn from each other as well as from her, because she believed children have important things to learn from each other. She talked about "the kinds of skills kids get from talking in groups, and the information they contribute, talking about themselves and telling some wonderful things happening to them and enhancing their self-concepts." Jean's view of children as having wonderful things to tell was expanded in later conferences and in classroom events that illuminated her view of children as sources of learning for adults. Later she said, "We all have some learning to do from each other," expressing her underlying view that we are all resources with practical knowledge.

When Jean said, "We all have some learning to do from each other," the "all" was inclusive of all children and adults. Frequently in mainstreamed settings the learning is as occurring in only one direction, the benefits accruing only to the mainstreamed child. On one occasion, Jean recalled her experience the previous year with Linda, a girl with a mild condition of Down's Syndrome, who had been mainstreamed in her classroom. A few of the parents did not want her in the nursery group. In particular, Alison's mother expressed disapproval, which led to a strong protest over a minor incident in which Linda hit Alison over the head with a small car, hurting her briefly. Jean described the scene, in which Linda had become angry with Alison following a variety of rejections. Linda had raised the car as if to strike, pausing long enough for Alison to move away, but Alison sat passively as she saw Linda approaching. Jean did not intervene, because she had anticipated some move to protect herself by Alison. (In conference with Alison's mother, Jean commented that she saw a need for Alison to get support for being more active on her own behalf, not by hitting but by verbal protest or physically moving.)

Jean expressed to Jeff her concern that a number of the parents saw Linda's presence as evidence that, "It's really nice, what you're doing for Linda," instead of recognizing that everyone had some learning to do from this experience. Jean pointed out that labeling Linda as "that mentally retarded girl," as Alison's mother described her, had destroyed the mutual attraction that had surfaced in the classroom between the two girls when school began. Thus the episode was very frustrating to Jean because it resulted in Linda's being rebuffed, and it detracted from her work as a facilitator of classroom learning by drawing on the knowledge vested in every member.

Teachers have to face conflicts that arise as part of group living. Jean had faced one such conflict between Alison and Linda. Jean met it by deciding not to act; at other times she did act, for example, when Mickey was hurling tires. In both cases, she considered the possible meaning of the events to the children, rather than simply using her power to impose law and order.

DISCIPLINING

In all groups, conflicts arise from a variety of sources. At times the needs of an individual are in conflict with the needs of the group. There are times when transitions must be made, turns must be taken, and materials must be shared. At such times Jean showed awareness of her power, weighing any actions she might take against what the events might mean to the children.

Children's Meanings

In an early conference with Jeff, there is evidence of her concern with children's meanings, as she responds to Jeff's concern about managing group life smoothly enough for learning to take place. He did not want to become a teacher-puppeteer, but in his early weeks he was searching for ways to run effective group meetings in which the conversation flowed well. First was the challenge of getting the children into a circle with everyone comfortable, and then getting their attention. Marcia was presenting a problem because she often talked to her neighbor when the children were expected to participate in group, not private, conversations.

JEFF: What if you just sit there and go, "You're making too much noise," you know, "Marcia, would you move over here?" And she doesn't move. Then, I hate to come to these scenes where you have to grab them and put them over there, and then . . . what happens? They hop right back. Then what happens?

JEAN: I don't know; then what happens?

JEFF: Those are the worst . . . times.

JEAN: When you can't get her to be quiet? Um . . . I guess, you were mentioning the instance where you worked in a fourth-grade class and the teacher said to the children that what they had to say wasn't important anyway. . . .

Jean had numerous options available to her, including quick tips, but she chose to move Jeff's concern into the framework of Marcia's talking as communication, reminding him of his concern when the fourth-grade teacher had been dismissive of the children's talk.

Although he would need to ask Marcia to be quiet and give her the reason, Jean was conveying what she believed to be critical in how the behaviors were understood. Marcia thought that she had something that must be said. As a teacher she acknowledged this even though she would impose a constraint on it, "Tell Angela at snack, please, we need to hear about how the bird feeder works now."

The Ripple Effect

Jean's perspective on power is elaborated in the following conversation with Jeff. Jean's classroom was as orderly and harmonious as any I have encountered, but these qualities were not

objectives so much as anticipated outcomes of living well together.

When a child was disrupting the group, Jean said:

> Well, do I separate this child from the group? Do I remove
> him from the other children? Then the implications of
> separating that child—you know, the whole scene where you
> say, "You're not ready to be with us," and the child gets
> removed, I mean—[makes fearful noise]—Wow! It's public at
> that point! Not private—where you're going over and giving
> them your opinion of what they're doing, and whether it's
> something you're going to tolerate. . . .
>   If you were there and you were yelling at someone,
> Marcia would be quiet. I could assure you that if you were
> yelling at Robin for doing something, Marcia would not say
> a word—she'd watch and she'd listen and be attentive, um,
> all of the eyes are always on you.

Jean is fully aware of the power implicit in the teacher's
position, of the ripple effect when a highly charged event occurring between one teacher and one child has meaning for all
the children and adults in the classroom.

Raw Power

Jean seemed particularly concerned that as a teacher she
should not use raw power with the children. Power struggles
with children were abhorrent to her. They seemed to occur
minimally because she insistently searched for the child's intention or "what kinds of signals" were being given. She did not
seem threatened or insulted by their acting-out behaviors, which
perhaps freed her energies to puzzle over what meanings the
events had for the children.

Below she discusses her feelings about clashes between children and their teachers.

JEAN: There was an instance where Mickey got into a literal
tug of war with an assistant teacher over a book and they were sitting there tugging back and forth with the book, which I think is tragic
when teachers get into a battle of wills with children.

JEFF: Yeah, oh . . . terrible . . .

JEAN: Um, and it took a while to undo. He was sitting on her lap, and he turned the page, and he was very surprised—it was one of these not-very-durable paperback books—and that page tore. And I guess she gave him some sort of a look and he got some attention for the page having torn, and I don't know if he necessarily does it for attention. I don't mean to be saying that. But—he looked at her, and saw her respond, and he took the page and was holding it between his fingers; he hadn't torn it but he was holding it like he was about to. She'd say, "Don't tear that, Mickey," and he'd look at her and grasp the book, and before long they were both tugging on the book. So it took many instances to undo that, because for the next several times, every time Mickey came over to the circle, and it was time to look at books, he'd look around and find Jane, not anyone else, and he'd hold up the book, and pretend that he was going to tear the pages.

JEFF: What'd you do with that?

JEAN: Well, in that instance I told her to stay very far away from him, and I sat next to him, um, and it really didn't happen anymore. I'd look at a book with him, and turn the pages very carefully. I guess there was one instance where he went to tear the page, and I said, "Mickey, please don't tear the page or we won't be able to look at the picture," or something simple like that, and it kind of did away with it.

But sometimes it's really difficult to see what they're looking for; what kinds of signals they're giving. . . .

Time With, Not Time Out

Sometimes Mickey's signals were misread or missed, and his acting out became too much for the class. Then Jean removed Mickey from the group. She did not think of this as "time out," which is a behavioristic technique used by adults as a way of punishing children. She thought of this being separated from the group as a chance for him to have time with another adult living through his distress with him and helping him move out of it. This reflected her belief that children were bent on making the best sense they can out of their lives and that it was her job to assist them, appealing to their conscious awareness and strengths.

Safety

Although the power vested in her as a teacher concerned Jean, she was not afraid of using it for what she considered to be safety issues.

One of the mothers had told Jean of an accident in her neighborhood, involving a child and a lawnmower, "So tell those kids to stay away from lawnmowers."

JEAN: She was very upset. She was on her way to the hospital, because it was her neighbor's child. So we talked about it today, and the children's response was very interesting. You know, I went into my human drama routine where you talk about how dangerous it can be—not so they're scared, but to impress upon them that it can be really dangerous. . . .

JEFF: Did you bring up the specifics?

JEAN: Yeah. And maybe, "Yes, you'd better be scared about that lawnmower. It can really hurt you." I didn't tell them the details, but I said, "Sometimes people put their hand under the blade, and the blade cuts into their hands." And one of the children, I think Marcia, said, "Yeah. It can chop your hand off." And Mickey, of all people, said, "I'd get another one." And it was like: "No. You *don't* get another one." Again, keeping that serious tone.

JEFF: Probably thinks when he runs in the road he's going to get a new body.

JEAN: Yes—and they see it on TV—you know, the bulldozer comes, flattens you, and you spring back up. So that's why I guess I'm so concerned about superheroes, and telling them, "No, these aren't real people."

INFLUENCE LIVES

She was not naive about the influence of teachers on children's attitude formation in terms of both how they see themselves and how they conceptualize their world. Young children are particularly vulnerable to the expectations of significant persons in their lives, who have the power to support their development in positive and lasting ways or to stamp out their uniqueness and leave labels in its place. Jean knew how easy it was to develop expectations about children which they tended to fulfill.

Expectations

She told Jeff she caught herself one day thinking, as she saw a spoon in the paint, "Mickey must have been over in the paint again." She told him of an incident when a child threw plastic blocks so that they flew everywhere. She told them sternly, "Don't ever do that again." Several of the children listened as Robin asked, "Who are you saying that to?" to which Jean responded, "The person knows who I'm talking to." Jean concludes:

> The other children are very aware of what's happening. It's easy to attach unpleasant things to children. Like the class tattletale . . . I think there are some teachers who develop that—some children who watch what's going on, whenever there's a commotion. . . . If you say to them, "What happened?" I think that can develop the tattletale syndrome in them . . . yet there are times when you can say to a child, "Gee, did you see what happened?" In certain situations, maybe positive ones: "It looks so bright and cheery over here." Involving children that way . . .

Jean seemed conscious that human beings can be pushed into roles that imprison rather than free them: the class clown, the scapegoat, the goody-goody student, and so on. With Johnny, Mickey, and Marcia, in particular, this was evident, as she worked at not permitting them to be labeled "troublemaker," "unpredictable," and "hyperactive," or "bossy," respectively, adjectives that elicit certain predictable adult responses. These tend to move rapidly to controlling instead of interpreting behaviors less judgmentally, thus coming closer to the child's intentions through understanding, although not necessarily condoning them.

In the following conversation, the focus was on the influence of expectations and the powerful way they codify experiences and human beings. Jean reminisced about Joshua in one of the other groups:

> At one of the seminars, the students were mentioning how much Joshua wanders away, on walks, won't stay with us at all—intentionally (my impression) and one day it was particularly dramatic. Just, "Joshua, stay over here, Joshua,

Joshua, Joshua." Finally, all the kids were going, "Joshua, come over here, Joshua!" The next thing you know I was holding Joshua's hand and kids in the class were looking back and going, "Joshua, Joshua, Joshua!" "Joshua's lost, where did he go?" *But he was right there holding my hand.* So they really had no sound evidence, but they had picked up on those expectations.

Attitude Formation

Jean had a concern shared by Jeff that teachers should not impose their own prejudices unthinkingly on children. This conversation spoke to this:

> JEFF: Mm—someone said it looked like I had fingernail polish on. . . .
>
> JEAN: Said to you? [laughs]
>
> JEFF: Yeah—you didn't hear that. . . . Donald—
>
> JEAN: What did you say?
>
> JEFF: I don't know [laughter]—that one caught me. . . . hmm.
>
> JEAN: Did you say yes or no?
>
> JEFF: I didn't really say yes or no; I said—I just said, "It does?"

JEAN: They do look shiny—and what if there were a boy in the class who did have polish on his nails, and you looked at the child, kind of askance—[draws in breath] "I don't have polish on my nails!" . . .

> JEFF: Yeah! That was my first—that was my initial reaction—in my head.

JEAN: Because one of the kids in the other class—Brian—has two sisters, and his sisters always polish his nails pink, red . . . all those colors.

> JEFF: I was thinking about that—yeah, 'cause my first reaction was [draws in breath], "Of course I don't have nail polish on" [laughter].
>
> JEAN: "What do you mean?" [laughter] We have to be so guarded all the time about everything we do. . . .
>
> JEFF: Yeah. We do! Right.

JEAN: And then we teach them to respond to affect, and—or not teach them to respond to affect, but we try and make them sensitive to affect, and then they pick up on it and they use it very quickly, and we communicate a lot to them. You might have tried to be as controlled as you could, and maybe in your language say, "Well, they do look shiny, but. . . ."

JEFF: I think that's what I did. . . .

JEAN: But your face might've been communicating to them, "Oh! I would never wear polish on my nails," or "Yes, I would wear polish on my nails," whatever the case may be.

JEFF: Right. Well, I think that's about what happened [laughter]. . . . I was trying to say something, but. . . .

JEAN: So many mixed messages. . . .

Teaching was never simple to Jean or to Jeff. Both highly self-evaluative, they listened for the reverberations of their values and beliefs in the minds of impressionable though resilient and dynamic children.

That she respected children's seriousness as learners did not mean that she was unaware of their vulnerabilities as immature persons, dependent on the significant adults in their lives. She never talked about herself as a role model, but she understood clearly that through the relationships she built in the classroom, she played an influential role. She thought a great deal about her influence on children's attitudes, particularly in areas where there was potential for clashes with the family. In a seminar with the student teachers she expressed her belief that school was a place where children should be given alternatives but that they should be presented as such, always in terms that are developmentally appropriate.

Conflicting Values

Jean had no pat answers to the dilemmas that arose when children came to school with different ideas and values. As in many classrooms, two subjects could be predicted to arise each year: food and guns. In common with many teachers of young children, Jean believes that junk food should be limited in, and preferably absent from, children's diets. She encourages fresh vegetables, fruit juice, and natural foods for snack time. But one of the parents owned a doughnut store and generously supplied the school with doughnuts. Jean said, "What do you do? You're saying these doughnuts are not so good for people? And it's his father's business?" She tried not to frighten the children as she said laughingly, "All your teeth will fall out if you eat them." Her compromise, talked over with the parents, was to limit the doughnuts to occasional treats.

Jean was aware of the conflicting values in our society about guns. In some early childhood settings, teachers do not permit toy guns. Jean was not pleased to see children bring toy guns to school because they can so easily lead to fighting and destructive behavior. However, she did not forbid them. She encouraged the children to put the guns away and used redirection to the interesting activities of the room. But she was aware of individual differences in terms of the meaning of guns and knew that the clue to understanding these was observation, listening, and learning what the gun meant to a particular child. Johnny continued day after day to bring in a toy pistol and would not be separated from it. Jean talked with his parents and found that his father, in common with many families in the area, was a very keen hunter. Jean invited him to talk to the children about hunting, including precautions, care, and his objective. Following the visit, Johnny, as Jean put it, "had told what he wanted to tell because it was an important part of family life." After this, he left the gun at home.

Facing up to the complexities of a diverse society with many changing values, Jean did not function in isolation. She talked with and listened to the children, the students, the parents, and other adults. She used consultation, deliberation, and reflection. And she weighed the effectiveness of her teaching in the lives of children through closely observing and recording the ways they were growing.

OBSERVING

Jean inducted Jeff into an important corollary of her belief about the complexity of children as seekers of meaning—the need to observe their behaviors over time:

I think one difference that we talked about a bit right after
class was being sure to put yourself in a place where you
can be strategically located, where you can see everything
that's going on. And to stay involved with whatever you're
doing with that child, or group of children, but yet, remember to look up—to have divided attention. And if there's an
instance where a child's doing something, or having a conversation, and it's really important that you hear what it is,
it's best to move aside and to take that time to listen, or to
remove yourself from the classroom.

The message here is that the teacher needs to be tuned in to the
worlds of children revealed in their actions and words, that
these worlds are interesting, significant, and sometimes in crisis.
These ongoing observations determine when the teacher needs
to center on a particular child or group and give concentrated
attention.

When to watch, whom to watch, and what guidance to offer concern Jeff as they do Jean. She echoed for him the perspective of Dewey: "Only by watching the child and seeing the attitude that he assumes toward suggestions can we tell whether
they are operating as factors in furthering the child's growth, or
whether they are external, arbitrary impositions interfering with
normal growth" (Dewey, 1960, pp. 129–130). This belief in
observation over time was an essential part of teaching to Jean.
It was rooted in her view of children as active inquirers with both
short- and long-term agendas.

The concept of observation over time as an integral element
in program design and assessment is not easily taught or practiced. One student speaking of teaching said, "I feel I should
know what I'm going to do before I do it." The reluctance to
be a part—a planned, prepared part—of a process is not surprising, in view of the technical bent of our society in which work
becomes increasingly proceduralized and measured, as Schön has
pointed out.

Jean's faith in observation was queried when the psychology
students first arrived. They came from working on very specific,
preset programs with children in the psychology clinic. In her
own words:

So many of the students ask when they first start, "Well, what do I do when I start tomorrow? What do I say? What do I do? Where's my script?" Well, there is no script. I discuss the children with them, and encourage them to sit back and relax, enjoy the children, and interact naturally with them. I tell them, "If you do something horrendous, I'll let you know" [laughs].

Beyond Surface Observables

Jean met with her students daily, informally, and weekly in a planned two-hour session. She assisted them in coming to an understanding of materials and methods, but her major thrust was toward opening their eyes to the satisfactions, certainly uneven, of learning to see the growth and development of puzzling but purposeful young humans creating their own worlds. She hoped to move them beyond the surface observables as she herself refused to be seduced by them. Like most teachers, she strove toward attaining a sense of harmony and order in the classroom, but she knew that orderliness in itself is not enough. She looked beneath the surface for the "hidden curriculum" in terms of its meaning for the children, whom she chose not to condition. One morning, she had striven for and attained an orderly transition between the classroom and the gymnasium for a group of children, including Mickey, but she was dissatisfied with the way in which she effected this. It was not enough for her that a strategy "worked."

Jean had planned three activities, two in the classroom and one in the gymnasium. The group was to divide into three and take turns participating in each of the activities; Jean let the children work out which group they would join first. Volatile in many transition periods, Mickey was upset when his turn came last, because he was left with no choice but to stay in the classroom when he wanted to go to the gymnasium. Despite this setback, he did settle back to play quite steadily and with concentration. As the 30-minute period of gymnasium for the others ended, Jean began preparing the children in the room for their turn. Mickey demurred. Now he did not want to go. Jean, in a very enthusiastic tone, said, "Oh, but Mickey, Marcia will be there and it'll be such fun." He went.

Later she raised this with the students in seminar, indicating that she felt she had been manipulative. They were puzzled by her reaction. "But it worked!" In the long discussion that ensued, Jean's thinking surfaced, as she sketched out an option she might have taken. She would have preferred to have told Mickey directly that it was time for him to go to the gymnasium, "in five minutes," not yet adding Marcia's presence there as a "rewarding social incentive." His reaction might have been tearful, noisy, and enraged, but she knew she could live through that with him and that these rages were becoming briefer in duration. Agreeing how difficult changes were, they could then have walked over to the gymnasium together. He could have discovered Marcia there, and Jean could have helped him put his experience into words. She also acknowledged that some days when she was tired, she did not want to work through his rages with him and would try to avoid them by being sure he was not left among the last to choose activities.

FEELINGS

Making sense out of life is not a smooth or bland process. Jean was aware of her own strong feeling and believed that young children, invested in their learning and living, experienced just as wide a vicissitude of feelings, which needed recognition and support. She talked with Jeff about working with children's feelings as an ongoing part of classroom life so that when a child says, "My mom was angry," it is important to take time to find out, "What makes your mom angry?" Jean also talked about showing children how she feels, "so that when I look at them, and I put my hands on my hips and my face is scowling they know that it's something they shouldn't be doing. . . . then I try to explain why."

Jeff discusses his discovery that he needed to express more strongly to the children his feelings when they ran on to the campus roads or walks. He acknowledges the anger he felt on a few occasions, but more generally a sense of being scared for what might happen to the children. Like a method actor learning to use feelings to convey feelings to an audience, Jeff is moving into the component of teaching that is akin to acting, which Jean supports, since dramatized events can speak to humans in powerful ways at all stages of development.

He tries to sort out for himself the welter of feelings he had when Mickey left the group and ran out in the road:

> JEFF: I mean, there's a little anger, but, you know, you really—you—you're scared for them! You know—it's scary; someone runs out in the road—there must be a car right there. Um, so in that case, yeah—you try to put on a very angry face, and make your voice sound very angry . . . without really being . . . you know, all that angry, but. . . .
>
> JEAN: Mmmm. Or some sort of different emotion. I'm using more words in the classroom—like concerned—"I'm very concerned about that" and using a kind of frowning face. So that they hear different words—I find myself getting frustrated when you say to a child, "How do you feel? or, "How does that make you feel?" and everything makes them feel "good" or "bad." It's either yes or no good or bad. . . . I want them to use different words, and I think we can—provide them with those different words, in relating it to experience and affect. . . .
>
> JEFF: That—and that, always—never ceases to amaze me—they do pick up those words, and use them, and they come out with big words. . . .

Jeff joined Jean in marveling at the complexity of young children as his observations and discussions led him to differentiate and describe "the 14 little stories" being written in the classroom. He lived through the experience of having to remind young children many times about whose turn it was to talk and having to highlight what was said. And he made a discovery that was key to the effectiveness he attained as discussion leader at the group meetings:

> Well, that's another thing: When you're saying something that interests them, you've got a better chance of having them quiet and listening. That's why . . . I think I have to be really organized in my group discussion—you know, ready

to go. Although I think you ought to be flexible, too, hear what they say and respond to that.

Jeff recognized the science of educational programming in the classroom and, with Jean, believed that discipline grew out of the power of curriculum in conjunction with the surging need to learn that is in young children. This had been confirmed early in her teaching and became part of her practical knowledge. Early in our sessions, she recalled her first substitute teaching job after she had received her A.A. degree. She went "cold" into a substitute teaching position in a cooperative nursery school that had built a reputation for its minimally controlled chaos. The parents "on duty" settled back to watch her, a new gladiator in the arena of early childhood, as they sipped their coffee.

When Jean arrived, the children and parents had been locked out for 20 minutes. After the door was unlocked, the parents went to the kitchen to make coffee, and the children "climbed the walls" as she made a circle of chairs and selected a book. To the amazement of the mothers (and to Jean's relief) the children, even the "biter," came and sat in the chairs. The story interested them, and from then on it was a good morning. This stayed in her memory as the first time she experienced fully the power of the educational program to speak to young children and bring them together. Some more of her beliefs about the educational program are presented in the following chapter.

4 Jean's Views of a Sound Educational Program

The education program set the stage on which Jean's values and beliefs about children, teaching, and education were played out. In this chapter the focus is upon what meanings the program supported and on how this was done, as well as upon the room it supplied for encouragement of the holistic growth of the children and adults as persons and as group members.

Jean's class was engaged in activities to be expected in sound programs for young children. They dictated stories, read them, cooked, painted, built with blocks, talked with each other and interesting guests such as musicians and health personnel, made gifts for each other and their parents, studied plants, cared for pets, learned numbers, sang many songs, danced and played active games, and took several carefully planned trips. But piercing beneath the layer of observable events lay Jean's intentions, hopes, and ideas, which defined what depth education had, what values were ascribed to its various components, and, consequently, what was available to be absorbed to varying degrees by the children, their parents, and other adults connected with the setting.

The sessions lasted 3 hours, beginning with an hour or so of free play when the children made decisions about how they would use their time and with whom they would play. Jean and the other adults observed and interacted during this time, generally following the children's lead. Free play was followed by group meeting time when the children formed a circle, talked, and listened to each other and to Jean or Jeff. One agenda item for the meeting was an explanation of the teacher-planned table activities that followed the group meeting. Outdoor play, walks, or movement education in the gymnasium rounded off the morning, which ended with a story time in the room.

Consistently with her views of children and teaching, Jean

believed that the education program must be broad enough to induct children into the public, shared world of the formal disciplines, as well as to enlarge the private, unique meanings children were creating.

FORMAL KNOWLEDGE

Some educators think it pretentious to talk about teaching young children such disciplines as history, literature, and geography. However, Jean accepted Bruner's thesis that it is possible to induce learning in an intellectually honest way, provided the content is developmentally appropriate. She believed that their present learning should enable the children to live fully in what Whitehead called "the insistent present" but that it should also serve as a foundation for future learning. Consequently a trip to the supermarket offered a challenging experience in learning about landmarks, guessing where roads went, checking out the guesses, wondering why the mailbox was where it was—in other words, engaging in the beginnings of human geography, of finding out about the world. When her children had such experiences as these she believed it would help them to meet the subject of formal geography because they would then have a well of direct experiences from which to draw.

In common with Lucy Sprague Mitchell (1934/1971), she saw the children as young geographers, and she explored the environment at hand in the university, where much building was taking place. Words cannot convey the sense of relish and intellectual aliveness that flavored the conversations on this topic between Jean and Jeff.

Jean was aware of the satisfactions derived from drawing on firsthand experiences and connecting them with formally organized knowledge. As this challenge continued to intrigue her, she attempted to invent such connections between the lives of those in the classroom and the disciplines.

In an age when curricula come advertised and prepackaged, many teachers have lost opportunities to invent some aspects of their educational programs themselves. In Jeff's previous placements, he had observed the teachers following preset curricula, so it was refreshing to him to discover that within himself and his experience lay worthwhile educational program content.

Personal Experience

Jeff grew to see how the events of one's own life could give special meaning to the educational program. Initially, as pointed out earlier, he found group discussions difficult. He made careful plans, but he did not at first fuse them with the children's first-hand experiences or his own life. Early in the fall, he saw geese flying over the campus from the northlands, a moving sight that he recounted to the children, who formed a rapt audience for once. It was in a sense a revelation for him, a practical demonstration of the view that the educational program is a valuable forum for sharing aspects of what has meaning for us as persons. Jeff's experience with the migrating birds potentially contributed to the children's lifelong study of nature.

Jean and Jeff explored connecting everyday experiences with broader frames of reference that might deepen the children's intellectual development. On one occasion, at the end of May, Jeff planned to substitute teach for Jean for a day. He was going to make pizza with the children because, on his weekends, he worked as a pizza chef.

JEFF: I was trying to think—you know, Margaret asked me to write up what I hoped to achieve—you know, I was thinking of objectives.

JEAN: Behavioral objectives . . . ?

JEFF: Not strict behavioral objectives but—you know—where I was going—and it's kind of hard to—specify, I find. You know, if I'm thinking of a lesson for my social studies class, a sixth-grade lesson, you can say "work on writing skills. . . . "

JEAN: Because they're specific content . . . ?

JEFF: They're more specific! We're talking about making pizza, and when I took the pictures at work, a few of the guys there asked me, uh, you know—"Are you really gonna teach about making pizza?" They thought I was really crazy. . . .

Many share the view of Jeff's colleagues that pizza making does not belong in school. Such critics would raise no question about time spent underlining on a ditto words or pictures a child already knows. Images of still, silent, obedient children are as strongly held as is the view of valid knowledge as a commodity available only from sanctioned, certified sources.

When Jean asked Jeff what he thought the children might learn from the experience, Jeff recognized that it was a social studies experience that would broaden the children's view of the. work world and the wider community, as do trips to the firehouse and the supermarket. He was pleased and became reflective when Jean commented that what was especially important to her was that he was a significant person in the children's lives, that they needed to learn that he not only worked with them but did other things, too. Young children do not deal easily with the notion of multiple roles, as teachers can attest who find children consistently, year after year, believing that they live in the schools where they teach. Children struggle to enlarge their perspective, and Jeff and Jean searched for ways to help them do this that drew on firsthand experiences.

Their conversation on the pizza event continued:

JEFF: A couple times when I've come back this semester they've wanted to know what I've been doing, when I'm not there. So another thing I wanted to bring in was one of the things I'm doing when I'm not here—they'd be interested in that aspect of it, you know, a person that they just see—only here—"What else does he do?"

JEAN: "Does he sleep?" "Does he live in a house?"

JEFF: Yeah.

JEAN: Before you came when I said that we'd be having a visitor, and even today when we talked about it—I started telling the children that this person is a teacher, and when he's not a teacher, he's a chef, and he makes pizza. And then I tried to change the wording around, and be more careful about presenting it. "This person is a chef; this person is a teacher. When this teacher isn't teaching, he does this. . . . " So that they get the concept that people can be many things at different times, and you do different things at different times. Not that—when—I don't know, maybe it's kind of a moot point—um, but that you still are a teacher, and that you still are a chef, even though you're not doing something related to that. So that when their dad goes off to work he's still their dad, or when the business executive comes home he's still the business executive, but his role becomes different, depending upon the setting he's in. So that the children's roles also become different, depending upon the setting they're in. When they're at school there are different expectations, when they're at home there are different expectations, when they go to ballet school there are different expectations, when they're at tumbling; so they see that people are the same, and have different roles and different functions. Maybe the wording I use is not necessarily that important, but I, uh . . . sometimes I think that it *can* make a difference, so I try and make that distinction, or try and think about how it sounds to the children: "Well, he's not a teacher, now he's a chef," or "When you're here, you're a teacher, so therefore you're not a chef—well, no, you're still a chef, but—this is what you're doing at this particular time. . . . " [laughter] Chef Jeff . . .

JEFF: And the name rhymes!

JEAN: Right [laughs]. Well, I told you when I told them that the person that was coming was a teacher and a chef, they just knew it had to be Jeff, because *Jeff* rhymes with *chef*, and that is—they knew! [laughs] I almost felt like having someone else come in, just to show them, "Ha! Ha! You think you're so smart" [laughs].

JEFF: So they—made the chef's hat. . . .

Both sociological and psychological learning were available for the children as they became aware that Jeff was a teacher and chef. In fact, they absorbed with pleasure later the fact that he was soon to become a husband. They might have discovered that even as he worked as a chef, he thought about them and about bringing them a pizza. The connectedness and complexity of life were brought to their attention, held their interest, and later nurtured their play.

Integrated Academics

Inextricably bound in with their social studies learning was prereading, a play with the words *Jeff* and *chef*. A project in which the children made chef's hats involved comparison, which is central to the concept of measurement. This integration of the academics as ongoing, relevant aspects of the educational program that Jean and Jeff valued was illustrated in the following extract of their dialogue about the hats:

JEAN: I loved the one that Marcia made—she was over there stapling and stapling—I saved it to show Margaret—and eventually—did you tighten it up, or did someone else?

JEFF: I did . . . so it would fit—she had about six pieces of paper.

JEAN: But their image! I thought their image was great—you know, they made the little ones, and a couple of weeks before they had been taking little strips of paper and stapling them, and putting them on top of their heads for crowns, but Marcia knew that that little thing just wouldn't fit on your head, because you're a bigger person—so she got three or four sheets of 9 by 12 paper and stapled them around . . . [laughs]. I think she was surprised that it kind of dropped down over your waist [laughs].

JEFF: I think she was! Because I held it about here, and then it dropped!

JEAN: She was persistent on it, though. . . .

In Jean's mind, Marcia and the other children could be trusted to engage and persist at worthwhile tasks undertaken through their own initiative. But they were not acting in a void.

PLAY

Jean valued the knowledge and skills all must share to become educated, but she wanted to provide for the unique dimensions of the person, too. She trusted that given free time and flexible support the education program could offer such provisioning.

Because she gave priority to play when children followed their own purposes, intent on making their own interpretations, breaking into the play to direct other activities, such as shared song or story times, was not done casually but deliberately. Jean looked for a sense that the group was ready for the next move. If children had to be disrupted in their play, she would quietly discuss this with them and let them know that there would be more time later. There was no throwaway time in this classroom or outdoors for "just playing."

Valuing Play

In one of our conversations, she talked about play:

Trying to make the decision of when to start group meeting time, when do you interrupt their play? Trying to see if there's a point where children are moving around, to catch them in transition, so as not to interrupt what they are doing.

Jean thought about times to intrude on their play in terms of her plans for the program. "When do you switch your objectives or redirect your thinking? As opposed to redirecting the children's thinking?" There was not an automatic adherence to teacher-made, advance plans but a balance between play she read as significant and experiences she planned as significant. This seemed to reflect her valuing of children's play and her comprehension of its potential.

In the following conference with Jeff, Jean talked through some of her thinking in relation to her observation of Jeff that morning. He was trying to get the group assembled for group discussion, but Mickey, busily trying to tape a picture he had made onto the wall, was ignoring his urging. Jean said:

I guess to me it just posed a dilemma in trying to decide what I might do, because of the particular child—because it was Mickey—because he was showing an interest in the room . . . being very involved in what he was doing immediately. Two children passed him by, and he showed them the picture, so there were lots of social skills involved, also. So I guess as I saw that, I was trying to think of what I would do.

Significant Learning

Perhaps the following extracts from a representative morning will help to illustrate what Jean saw as significant meanings children create for themselves and for each other and how, as the planning, assessing adult teacher, she designed an education program to support a variety of learning.

It was a cold February morning, and I arrived just after most of the children, delayed as I groped along the icy walks that were so enjoyable to them. Children were in different parts of the room in control of where they were. I caught some of the serious talk between Marcia and Simon, who were arguing about the work of the Easter Bunny:

MARCIA: [very definitively] The Easter Bunny puts the eggs in your basket when you go to your mommy's room to eat breakfast.

SIMON: [diffidently, unsure] Sometimes . . . [more assertively] but sometimes he hides them . . . like?

The Easter bunny will resurface in a debate involving more of the children, who raise some questions and philosophize about their meaning. In the meantime, I heard this snatch of conversation:

DONALD: We haven't found out what we're going to do.
ROBIN: I know what we're going to do today. I see something over there.

In referring to the notice in words and pictures of the day's work on the bulletin board, Robin was giving Donald an early lesson in information retrieval.

Jean told Pat and Robin that she needed to make some big circles and wanted to find something to use to make them. They looked puzzled. Jean hauled over the garbage lid, and their looks changed to delight. Jean cut as Pat, Robin, and quiet Angela watched.

PAT: The other day I bought a pizza.
JEAN: I bought a rectangular pizza the other day.
PAT: I cut like that, Jean, with my big scissors. My mom helps me.
ANGELA: That looks like a big pizza, doesn't it?
ROBIN: [as Jean continues cutting] You got a lot of circles.

Robin counted them as Jean went for more materials. Often the children did not respond at once to new vocabulary such as *rectangular*, but the word resurfaced later. At this point there were 10 children in the room, decision makers in free selection of activities. So far in this morning of free play, the children within my earshot had not been wasting time. They had been focused by Jean or by each other on a range of cognitive activities such as counting, noting sizes, and hearing new information or a new word. The rest of the free play hour went by; block buildings were made; children painted and talked.

Following this, however, the children were called together for group meeting time, which centered on peanut butter, relating to a planned table activity to follow. The activity involved shelling the peanuts, many of which were popped into mouths, an accepted part of the experience. But to return to the group meeting, some of the discussion went as follows:

MARCIA: Robin, don't put your finger in it [the mixer]. It'll cut your hand off. Kids should never touch sharp things.

KEVIN: [beaming] Not even knives?

ROBIN: [very seriously, time-on-task-oriented, to Jean] Are you going to give us the recipe?

Kevin gave Marcia some food for thought. She stared at him, perhaps nonplussed. Jean discussed ways of cracking peanuts and brought in a variety of seeds, expanding on their classification. At the end of the session she asked the children to observe the tulip bulbs and the corn seeds that were growing. Their reactions, full of drama and suspense, infected us adults. Children noted joyfully, "The one in the middle is the fattest," or sadly, "One hasn't done anything at all." Making cognitive discoveries about the seeds, an early science activity, came fused with feelings that were generally positive, even enthusiastic. Jean then moved on to a concern in relation to the calendar, connecting learnings about time with very personal experiences, birthdays.

Jean told the children that Simon's birthday was in February and that February was lost. Simon said, "I might find it!" while Marcia, pulling out the December page, declared, "I founded it."

When the children saw her hold up December, Jean asked if this word was *February*. She juxtaposed the words *February* and *December*. The children looked, but there was not much overt responding. Jean was not disconcerted by the lack of response. It reminded her that most of the children were still in a pre-reading stage. But she did want to give them the opportunity to see the different configurations made by *February* and *January*. The group meeting moved along. Marcia asked: "Is it time to get up yet? My feet are falling asleep." Jean told her to wiggle them. Donald commented on the blender to be used with the peanuts. Marcia told Donald to raise his hand, and she began to talk, but Jean said quietly, "Excuse me. I haven't finished what I need to say."

Following more discussion, which is related in the next chapter, the group meeting came to a close, and the children went to the three tables with peanuts on them. Mickey began eating voraciously, storm clouds gathering in his head because he had lost a new ring he had worn to school that morning. Peggy needed Sue's gentle assurance that it was all right to eat some of the peanuts, as she looked hungrily at the other munching mouths.

Robin decided he had had enough peanut shelling and went to the science corner to get a box of magnets. Several children watched him experiment as Sue helped him sort and classify materials that attracted or repelled or did nothing. Jean reminded them that the calendar was still lost, that Simon's birthday was coming and they would need it. Robin stopped his work. He said, enlisting Angela, "We're not playing anything. We're trying to find the calendar. Wanna do that?" Interestingly, he categorized his early science work on magnets as "play" and nonserious. Many adults in our culture, unfortunately, would have agreed.

Angela observed, "Somebody might have took it off the wall and put it under something." In a change of focus, they ran around chasing each other, which was not permitted in the small space of this room. Jean asked Robin quietly, "Did you find it yet, Robin?" She suggested new places to look, and he and Angela went off and found it where a child had hidden it. Jean gave them a card on which *February* was printed and asked them to find that on the calendar. She frequently posed these reading problems for the children, and each day as they grouped, they "read" the calendar, recipes, notes, and other written communications that were significant for them and caught their interest. The children taught each other reading, too, as will be shown later.

As noted earlier, the morning began with a discussion of the Easter Bunny, and this continued throughout the semester. When the children found ideas that meant something to them, they visited and revisited them over the months, putting to shame the myth of "short attention spans." These ideas often had philosophical and ethical bases. For example, Johnny challenged the notion of the Easter Bunny, his religious background having taught him to reject this imaginary animal and to center on the fundamental Christian perspective. The other children were outraged and wanted to know who brought the presents if not the Easter Bunny. They asserted that they had seen him at the Oakdale (sometimes called Oatmeal) Mall. Marcia, as usual, had the last word: "There *is* an Easter Bunny," with the telling afterthought, "Big grown-ups wouldn't fool little children." That stopped all of us in our tracks.

Children heard each other's ideas, and conflicts that arose were responded to with feelings and intellect as these young children drew on their own life experiences to make generalizations. As the children talked together, Jean heard their thinking. She did not feel compelled to move in and clear up misconceptions at once, because that would have encouraged the children to look at her as the source of all solutions. Instead, she stored up their comments so that in reflection she could think of ways of responding to them through the education program. Two central concepts emerged this particular morning, the Easter Bunny debate having to do with building respect for our rights to hold different religious beliefs and another having to do with human differences in relation to caring for or harming children, "fooling little children" as Marcia put it. These are not concepts for units to cover, but they are ideas that Jean viewed as part of the educational program throughout the year; in informal, one-on-one discussions and in group meetings and in the selection of which books to bring to the children, which persons to invite, and which community events to discuss.

The education program was open-ended. When the children

were discussing pizza, at the beginning of this observation, Jean introduced the new word *rectangular* once and let it lie. As with the idea of the Easter Bunny, the new word would come up later. Marcia's lecture clearly shared information, but Jean would not use it then. Peanut butter was an important curriculum element throughout the year. It was not an activity with a beginning, middle, and end.

PORPOISES AT PLAY

Much of this education program, in which all had something to contribute, was like porpoises at play. Ideas surfaced and vanished only to reappear in a new context later. It was such an unmechanical process that the lay onlooker might label it unpredictable, but that would be to discount the strength of children's needs to add to their store of knowledge even as they restructure it and the teacher's ability to grasp and nurture a many-leveled curriculum. Sybil Marshall (1968) in her one-room country school conceptualized her curriculum as a symphony with major components and side themes. This analogy signifies the rich complexity of learning that is not always linear, not always sequential, not always hierarchical so that self-generated insights and understandings can come into play as children learn together but in their own unique ways.

Sometimes Jean reintroduced ideas; sometimes the children did. Jean previously had asked the children how they thought peanut butter was made. Pat suggested putting peanuts in a jar with water, and the other children agreed. The only container at hand was a Coca-Cola glass, so they used this. Days passed, and a mess that was clearly not peanut butter resulted. Jean wondered why they thought this had happened. Johnny said, "Oh, it won't work . . . because it's a Coca-Cola jar."

Jean viewed Johnny as one of her young scientists at work, moving from one hypothesis to the next. Testing the impact of the container became a part of the curriculum to be followed by seeing the actual process before their eyes and tasting it on their tongues.

Encouraging children "to use their own two eyes," she

regularly responded to, "What are we going to do?", which children asked of the planned morning events, by directing the children to look and see. Most of them come in with the same energy and interest one sees as children enter a museum for children or any well-planned nursery or kindergarten classroom. They could be characterized as explorers, safe in making their hypotheses because no one would fault them as failures or impose their own conclusions on them. They seemed imbued with feelings of empowerment that freed their energies and imagination. The view that they were knowledge builders as well as knowledge consumers seemed to be related to the sense of autonomy they evidenced in their room.

Planned Components

Porpoises-at-play is an image that contrasts sharply with the sequential, orderly small-step-by-small-step model of curriculum whose precision is so neatly controllable. Learning was not in one set of capable hands but was a community venture. It was not, however, random or hit-or-miss but was energetically undertaken by the children more or less spontaneously and by Jean more or less purposefully. Jean's plans were often shifted to meet inspirations and exigencies of the group life, so they had a spontaneous quality, but this grew out of extensive planning, past assessments, and reflective observations recorded and discussed with the teaching team.

Every observation revealed many planned components. On my last observation in May, Jean had bought a fresh pineapple for snack, the children had brought photographs of themselves as babies, and there was butcher's paper for drawing body outlines. Jean had set in motion a cavalcade of possibilities, which both she and the children explored.

I arrived at the same time as Johnny, who began telling Jean that he had eaten 400 pizzas. She joined in the joke and asked, quizzically, "All at the same time?" Johnny was convulsed with laughter at the nonsensicality of her question. Brad came in, noticed the pineapple on the table, and asked, "Is that what we're going to eat for snack?" Sue encouraged him to touch and smell it, which he did very seriously and deliberately. Angela entered

with her baby brother at the same time Stuart and his father came
in. There was a lot of movement and bustle, because Marcia had
come in with her grandmother and gone directly to Thumper's
cage to hug and greet him only to receive back a firm nip on her
buttock. She was screaming with outrage and pain. The skin was
not broken, but she wept as if her heart were. Stuart's father
continued to talk to Jean even as she attempted to console Marcia.
Kevin came in and went over to fill the water table with Sue.
When Marcia finished weeping, she, Brad, Johnny, and Stuart
went over to watch Sue, and there was much laughter about the
air bubbles.

Teaching on the Fly

Donald entered and joined Angela at a puzzle. Pat came in
full of purpose and told his toddler brother that he must go home
now, in a tone of authority and even smugness, as he surveyed
the humming workroom of this classroom. The twins made their
usual puckish entrance. Pat observed the pineapple, and Marcia
moved over to join him. They were talking about where it was
bought:

> PAT: Every store had 'em. Giant had them.
> JEAN: Do you think you'd see one at Bradlee's or K-Mart?
> PAT: Schuster's [which is a grocery store].
> MARCIA: Shoe store?
> JEAN: Sounds like a shoe store. Pat, do you think you'd find
>   one in a shoe store?
> PAT: Yeah!
> JEAN: A shoe store?
> MARCIA: [with a caught-you voice] At Schuster's.
> JEAN: Do you think you could get shoes at Schuster's?
> PAT: [laughing] No.

The children at the water table on the far side of the room chant:
> Shoe store.
> Shoe store.
> Schuster's.
> Schuster's.

Engaging with the children, having a word for their younger siblings and their parents, overseeing the room with its numerous activities, Jean found time on the fly to play with words, a "pre-reading lesson" for those who like to cut learning up into bits. Enjoyment of language and growing awareness of sounds, their fine junctures, were evident as Jean helped Pat move to express his thinking in a more differentiated way by refining his classification of stores and what may be purchased in them.

Earlier in the year Jean's beliefs about teaching language were evidenced as she talked to Jeff.

> You gave them a word—you used the word *delicate* when you were talking about the carrot plant. And everything about the way you were talking—the way you were holding the pot, the way you were passing it around, the other words that you used—gave them lots of other information about the word delicate. You used the word *thin*, you used the word *careful*, you used the word—trying not to touch the thin plant, that was just starting to grow, um, and I think from children hearing lots of those kinds of examples of us saying the word, and following it up with a little descriptor, not so much like a definition—but lots of other cues, so if you give them a word, and give them lots of other relating ideas, and making a connection with the main idea—for example, the concept of delicate—is that much more likely.
>
> I think you have a greater chance of reaching more kids with a particular concept if you're giving them lots of information about it. Um, sometimes I think people avoid using appropriate words with children, because they're afraid the children won't understand.

As the children worked on the sorting, sifting, and classifying activities in this workshop world of early education, Jean dipped in and out of activities, lifting the level of discussion in ways that revealed her valuing of the children's cognitive development.

One day the children were talking about Ronald McDonald's coming. Brad had said very excitedly, "next year." Jean commented, "Brad said 'next year'—that's a long time." The children looked at her, said nothing, and pressed on. Young children often mull over things and later surprise adults by recalling events long past. As teachers of young children can attest, feedback is often later, sometimes weeks later. Jean and Brad continued to talk about what he thought Ronald McDonald would do.

Building on their keen interest in Ronald McDonald, Jean raised a question with them about time. For young children time is elusive, but it is a concept that they are building and expanding, so that when they begin to grapple with its complexity it is surely a first step into the discipline of history. As the children become involved with their books about themselves, they made and read their first history book and had the opportunity to see the effect of time on themselves. This concept building, as noted earlier, pervaded the entire year.

Following this small conversation, Jean moved over to Marcia, who told her, "We're missing a lot of friends, you know. We're missing Robin." Jean informed Marcia that he was moving into his new home. Kevin smiled, told Marcia he loved her as he took a huge blob of paste and put it on a small piece of construction paper, and then left. Jean commented nonjudgmentally to Marcia that she wondered why Kevin used such a big lump of paste to put on his paper. Marcia looked blank for once. This musing with children was characteristic of Jean's teaching. She moved around the classroom, observing the children, commenting, questioning, and trying to understand what they were intent on doing. As noted earlier, it was often very hard to record what she was saying because she spoke to the children in a low, conversational tone, much of the time on a one-to-one basis.

On this same morning, the children looked at the photographs of themselves as babies. Mickey and Peggy, having spent years as foster children, had no such record, so more recent photographs had been substituted. Jean helped some of them trace their bodies on butcher's paper, an activity that they had done the previous fall and one that was repeated at the end of the year to help them see how far they had come, the differences in their physical selves over time. (The decision-making process of taking turns to be traced was discussed earlier.)

UBIQUITY OF FEELINGS

This activity elicited some anxiety from Simon. Towering about a foot above many of the children, he seemed a gentle and at times uncertain person. As he cut out his image, he accidentally cut off the finger. Quietly he mumbled, "Humpty Dumpty," to himself. When Johnny approached him he said, "Johnny, my finger's got a little bit cut off." Wordlessly, Jean put the masking tape within his reach almost simultaneously with Simon's saying, "I'm getting kind of dead. My finger's cut off."

Jean was busy with Pat and Johnny nearby, and Simon joined in a discussion about the T-shirts the boys were wearing—Smurfs, Pac-man, and Superman. Johnny spotted Simon's damaged image again and declared, "Looks like he got in a car crash." Jean countered with, "Looks like his picture did. His body looks fine to me."

At this, Simon smiled in a dreamy way, but his expression changed to high concern when Johnny jumped over his picture and he told him sharply, "If you keep doing that, I'm not gonna be your friend."

For Jean, the education program was not divided into activities that centered on cognition and those that were in the domain of feelings. She attended to Simon's expressed dismay about his broken body image, giving him the means to fix it and demonstrating her belief that he himself was really a whole person.

CHILDREN TEACH CHILDREN

Jean believed that the education program should give children opportunities to teach each other. Some days it seemed as if the children centered on concepts of measurement, reading or pre-reading, and what are called "academics." During one observation early in March the children seemed to be concentrating on teaching each other academics.

It was another gray day in a mild, sunless winter. Marcia was absent. Mickey, Peggy, and Brad had chosen to be in the housekeeping corner. Jean was straightening out the nails on the nail-board used for simple weaving. Peggy wanted the sponge from Mickey: "Now it's my turn." Mickey said, "Nooo . . . ," but he gave it to her.

The twins were giggling at the entrance of the room. Sue, the student teacher, kneeling at their level, made some suggestions. Robin told Jean about his skating lessons and his family's move to a new apartment. Brad was having something of a bad day. He went into the housekeeping corner after saying crossly in response to my greeting, "You're not my Mommy, damn." He picked up the telephone, "38–48–58. Hi, Mom. How are you? . . . " Student teacher Bud came up and asked him if he knew his telephone number. He talked with him about his new crayons. But Brad went back to "talk to" Mom.

Angela and Donald were comparing heights on the chart. The following observation left them looking stunned. "I'm bigger than you are." "I'm older than you."

Relationship building, making connections between age and size, is difficult at their age. Many educators believe that numerous encounters that puzzle and engage the children's thinking about such variables are the building blocks for concept formation when supported by a constructive teaching-learning environment.

One table had crayons, a mirror, and some photographs; the other table had peas in pods for children to shell. Peggy and Pat worked on this. Simon, Stuart, and Johnny were in the housekeeping corner.

STUART: Do you know how to tie shoes?

JOHNNY: Sorry, I don't know how.

STUART: [to Danny, who is drawing on the blackboard] You're making all legs. An octopus?

JOHNNY: I forgot what I was making.

Stuart turned to Johnny for help but was politely refused. In the process of Johnny's experimenting with shapes, critic Stuart had some words on the subject that may well have focused Johnny on the gestalt of his lines.

Simon wrote his name on the blackboard. Johnny, Stuart,

and Simon talked about books they had at home. Pat listened. Johnny wrote his name on the board.

STUART: Johnny? Where's the *e*?

JOHNNY: There isn't any.

STUART: [very perplexed] But John-*ee*. John-*ee*. [singing] John-ee-ee.

The child of a graduate student, he said: "I gotta get going. I'm late for a class." He came back at once and asked with a beat, "Where's-the-*ee*? Where's-the-*J*?"

Jean brought the children's folders with their names on them and work in them (drawings, collage, dictated stories) on Johnny, Simon, and Stuart, and the children talked about how they wrote their names. Johnny said: "Hey! I write *Superman. Batman.*" Stuart corrected him: "You wrote *Batman* and *Robin.*"

Pat scribbled, whereas Stuart and Johnny printed. No opprobrium was attached to Pat's work by the other two boys. They seemed to have absorbed Jean's developmental perspective: First children experiment with lines and shapes, then they work at letters. The children were interested in words and intrigued by the illogic of spelling. (It is perhaps worth noting here that when I did most of the observations I did not single out what seemed to be the most interesting events. I sat quietly in a spot and recorded the events around me. Such conversations as the one recorded here were quite representative of those in other parts of the room and among other children, according to Jean and Jeff.)

As the morning continued, Jean encouraged Kevin to draw, but he declared, "I just don't want to," which she accepted, taking his hand to walk over and look at the children who were drawing. These children talked together about new self-portraits. They said things like, "I'm talking to myself," "This is me when I'm mad," and "This is me when I'm sick."

Sue talked with them about these feelings as Jean went over to Brad, who continued to look angry. His expression changed into cheerfulness when Jean asked if he would help at the flannel board. Stuart joined them silently. Interpreting his move positively, Jean told Brad, "There's Stuart. He came to see what

we're doing. He came to help us." Brad pressed pictures on the board, chanting away: "The moon goes up and up and up and up, up and up, up and up."
Simon and Johnny began building together:

SIMON: I wish we had pop-up books [pause]. How old are you?
JOHNNY: I'm five.
SIMON: [astonished] But I'm bigger!
JOHNNY: [with disbelief and resignation] Yeah! [I] can't believe it!

The concern with age and size resurfaces in the above dialogue, child-initiated cognitive food for thought, possibly of the nature Piaget refers to as accommodative in the sense that it causes an upward shift in the structures of the mind. Jean wove in and out of different subgroups, listening and observing and working at helping the children engage in social interactions, conversing, giving information, raising questions, laughing, puzzling, an active, engaged inquirer.

This cavalcade of possibilities kept the children actively engaged. They seemed too centered on what they were doing as persons or in small groups to engage in conflicts for long or to enter the seductive lands of superhero play. When Simon turned on the play TV to "see" the Dukes of Hazard, he was joined by a couple of other boys, who seemed to be revving up for some wild action. Angela, however, proposed in an unusually firm tone for her that they all make popcorn, so they became busy with that and forgot the Dukes. Jean saw it as part of her work to provide activities that were constructive so that the children would not be seduced by the allures of Superman, the Dukes, and other violent influences.

TEACHERS/LEARNERS

Jean believed that the educational program was for everyone, including the adults; all needed to be teachers and learners. There were many occasions when children provided Jean, Jeff, and me with telling lessons that had significance and import for us. Of the numerous small encounters, there were two especially note-worthy times when we learned from the children. They were highlights, and we talked about them throughout the year. They became part of our repertoire of school events that were carriers of strong beliefs about children and other related areas. These were the kind of events of which we said afterward, "It made our day."

A flat recording of words cannot convey the joy in Jean's voice as she talked about a few moments she enjoyed with Kevin in March during group meeting. In contrast to the beginning of the preschool year, a time of restless mat sharing and brief ex-changes, group meetings now often resulted in informative dis-cussions. Jean discussed one such session:

> There was one instance with Kevin, when he had just started. We read a story—it was just so delightful. We were reading *The Three Wishes* and after the story we were talking about wishes, and I asked the children if they could have one wish what would they wish for? And some of the children are wishing they had diamonds and boxes of gold and things like that, and I came to Kevin . . . and I said, "Kevin, if you had one wish, what would you wish for?" And in his little Kevin voice, he says, "I'd wish for a *big* oak tree." And I said, "What would you do with your oak tree?" He said, "I'd stand under it and I'd shake it until all the leaves fell down on top of me" in this incredible voice; and all the children sat there and he had them captivated. And we were just, like, "Ah! How wonderful!" So when it came time for me, I said, "I wish that I could be under Kevin's oak tree with him when all the leaves are falling down." And he says, "Oh sure, it'll be so much fun!" (We laughed.) It was just so refreshing, from, you know, the diamond necklaces and jewels . . . that the children wanted. And looking at the dif-ferences in how children begin those attitudes and values, and how they—pick up on those things.

A number of small events led up to the second occasion when Jean and the rest of us learned a significant lesson from a child. In this case, it was Mickey who acted as teacher. Jean had brought in boxes for group meeting discussion. The children were talking to each other about Chicken McNuggets, and Jean waited for this discussion to conclude. She then showed the children the boxes and asked them, "What do you think is inside? Shall we see?" Mickey said in a staccato voice, "Open it." Having begun by tearing off a piece of the cardboard box sculpture the group had worked on, he had had a bad morning. It had been hard to calm him down. But he was sitting next to Jean in the circle, and he looked riveted as Jean held up a box:

> JEAN: What do you think is inside this one? Shall we see?
> MICKEY: Open it.
>
> [It contained cotton wool, which Mickey took out and then put back. Several children suggested smelling it.]
>
> MARCIA: Cotton! I knew it! Open the box.
> MICKEY: Lots and lots of boxes. Let me have a box. [To Robin] You got paint? I got box.

In these basic sentences, Mickey moved into a new realm of cooperative play. He was making one of his rare overtures, and he could not have chosen a more responsive partner.

Following the group discussion, half the group was going to the gym; the rest were going to paint and glue papers on the small boxes. Jean let the children choose their activity out of the two and wrote their names on a chart "so we'll know just where everyone is." When Peggy saw Mickey's name, she beamed. "Mickey-my-Mickey," she cried, while Mickey exclaimed with delight: "Peggy. It say Peggy."

Mickey had shown little interest in letters or drawing, so his delighted recognition of Peggy's name was a benchmark occasion. This was turning into one of those great mornings for Mickey and his teachers. He joined a small group of children at one table where there were paint and glue and proceeded to smear the paint over the table. Two steps forward, one step back! But as he smeared, he told himself, "So dirty . . . can't taste it . . . so dir-ty."

Jean asked them to think about the color they wanted to use. Mickey worked on his box and chanted a little song. When Jean noticed this she commented, "I heard you singing. Would you like some music? With the instruments or singing?" Seeming not to hear this, Mickey continued painting for a few minutes, then he washed his hands clean. He went over to Jean's boxes, opened one, and made a triumphant "Eureka" noise. Quickly, Jean came over to him joining his excitement, and asked him what he had found. In tones of discovery and triumph, Mickey announced, "Nothing."

Later Jean described her joy at his pleasure: "When Mickey was opening the boxes and finding nothing in them, I was thinking he opened them with such delight as if there were diamonds and jewels inside (you know, imposing an adult value!) and how nothing seemed to be the same kind of value, for him. It was, for him, just delight in finding nothing, and with himself."

In a society where consumership is a constant overarching value pressed home by the advertising industry's enormous talent and wealth, Jean found a respite from subliminal and overt messages to consume and a reminder that sources of human delight are available within ourselves.

Mickey's delight in the emptiness of the box culminated a morning of small triumphs for him: Peggy's pleasure in his name, Mickey's finding a pal in steady Robin, and his recognized capacity to choose not to eat the paint. We were all reminded that small recognitions of us as persons and the small steps ahead we take can be sources of wonder and delight in our lives.

Jean believed that children could be responsive partners in their own growth and development, that they had something important to contribute to adults: "We all have some learning to do from each other." This learning was at times an aperitif, at other times a meal that was nourishing to Jean as a person and a teacher. Memories of Kevin with his oak tree wish always brought us laughter and relief from tension. Mickey and his entrancement with an empty box pulled us back to the nature of delight and the falseness of its constantly being equated with consumable products.

This educational program reached out to all the human beings in the classroom, demanding their energies and efforts but offering them in return the chance to engage in sustaining and significant learning. Jean observed, recorded, and described this learning frequently and regularly with the children themselves individually and in groups, with the student teachers, and with the parents. She built carefully documented cases as evidence that all the children were engaged in educationally worthwhile pursuits in their own unique and shared ways.

It is time now to look at the children as a classroom group and to see what difference it made to them that Jean held the particular values and beliefs that have been discussed in these chapters.

5 Jean's Beliefs In Action

In some early childhood classrooms children go about their isolated pursuits, occupied, content, but not participants in a cohesive group, as Susan Isaacs (1971) noted half a century ago when she wrote that for children of 5 years "the group is little more than background for each child's individual activity" (p. 76).

The 14 children in this group did play parallel at times, but increasingly as the year progressed the "clumping" Jeff looked forward to occurred. The children became a cohesive group; they knew who belonged and who was missing on certain days. They taught each other and their teacher, and they learned. Most significantly, they incorporated as full members two children, Mickey and Peggy, whose special needs in many settings would be viewed as a burden and whom the children would learn to reject. Healthy groups can incorporate children who are different because they are characterized by a flow of interaction that is comparatively free of competition, invidious comparisons, and undue ritualization and rules. The ways in which Jean's group incorporated Mickey is discussed in this chapter.

In healthy groups, leadership is exerted as a liberating, not a dominating, force because it springs from positive, not needy, sources. Jean was the formal adult leader of this group; Marcia unquestionably was an influential child leader. The experiences of a child with special needs, Mickey, and of a "born leader," Marcia, are presented impressionistically as evidence of the impact of Jean's values and beliefs on the classroom and its human occupants.

MICKEY

The reader has met Mickey on several occasions in this book, but it is time to describe him in more detail. Mickey had unusually demanding needs. He lived in his latest foster home, having been

abused in his own family. He first came to the behavior management program of a special education setting in his fourth year.
At 5, clearly not able to participate in a formal kindergarten
program, he was sent to the nursery school, a small, waiflike
child with a puckish grin that appeared on various occasions.

Jean's advance notice about him informed her of the bare
details of his life. She was told he was "aggressive" and "unpredictable," with poorly developed language. Aggressive he
turned out to be, but, for Jean, children are not unpredictable.
Teachers are detectives, searchers for the meaning children are
imposing on their worlds, as adults impose meaning on theirs.
She felt she needed to find out the meaning to Mickey of his
experiences.

Mickey's Anger

In circle time on his first day Jean said, "He put his little
hands on my neck in a gentle grasp." She told herself, "Don't
panic. Don't let him think you think he's going to choke you."
She continued, "His facial expressions are priceless. His fingers
slowly left as I looked at him."

Mickey's entry to the group went well enough except that
he left the session with blue paint spattered all over his clothes,
which angered his foster mother. In the future, Jean was careful
to see that he did not work without being covered with aprons
to avoid his getting a negative reception at home. One day she
was planning to take the children out to a muddy field, so she
changed Mickey completely except for the new white hat he was
wearing. Jean could not believe her eyes when "he fell head first
into a mud puddle on his head with his white hat . . . like an
ostrich." He came up forlornly and said, "I fell in the mud."
Jean's sense of humor provided her relief as she laughed about
this, laughter that was empathic with, not isolating of, Mickey.

Early in November Jean said:

> We had taken the children outside and I was all set to
> give Mickey's "parents" this glowing report. I had tried
> telephoning them on the weekend. He's stringing sentences
> together, behaving marvelously, excited, interested, opened

up [Jean sounds excited, interested, and amazed]—
interacting with other children. When we opened up the
pumpkin there was the white mold. He was making all these
connections: "Spider? Web—spider?" So I was trying to get
in touch with his parents. All of a sudden, here we are outdoors, he starts knocking tires into children, knocking them
off their feet; so I say, "Mickey, please don't roll the tires,"
and he laughs and picks up a bigger tire.

In tones of disbelief Jean continues:

Not only does he go for a child, but a child who's on
the swing, and not only will he get the child on the swing,
but there's a teacher standing in front of the swing, so I'm
sure he had it thought out: If he pushed the tire just right,
knocked the child off the swing, the child would push the
teacher down so he'd get two for one. So I see it coming!
"Mickey, *don't* do that. . . . You can't play here," I say at his
level. He hauls off and slaps me in the face. I probably
deserved to be slapped by Mickey because I was on his case
about this tire.

So Jean took Mickey inside to play quietly alone. Later, at
circle time, Jean sat close to Mickey, because, she said:

When he has these incidents, they really spiral so I'm
sitting right there, so he won't hurt the other children.
Mickey is being the model child. He asks me, "You OK?
Feel better?" and strokes my cheek. I tell him very firmly,
"It still hurts. I don't want you to do that."

While understanding his anger and his feelings, Jean set
limits on his acting out, but they were limits that were explicitly
made to his conscious awareness. She was not thinking of re-
warding-punishing or extinguishing. She did not simply regard
these outbursts as meaningless. She saw reasons for his anger,
acknowledged it, but limited its expression. Jean was not con-
vinced that Mickey's impulsive behavior came out of the blue.
As a result, she scrutinized the environment for reasons, and she
speculated about his inner world. She put herself in his place with

empathy and recognized how she would feel. Jean felt keenly how Mickey experienced events.

Cause for Anger

Jean searched for places where the anger in Mickey built up. She knew that life in the foster home was not clear sailing; the journey to school on the bus was very poor preparation for entering a group, and then there was the dichotomy between the two learning environments: hers in the morning and the behavior management program in the afternoon. When Mickey hurled tires at everyone he could reach, he had his reasons. She had to control him, but she understood that it made sense to him. As his teacher, she searched for ways to communicate with the foster parents and with the behavior modifiers. She said on many occasions about a number of difficult situations that she did not want to seem too critical because she did not believe she had all the answers.

Searching for clues to infer the meaning of events to the children grew out of her view of them as human beings coming to each situation with a past history. Mickey's past was less available because he had lived much of his life in the homes of strangers, but Jean tried to imagine it. On one occasion in October, Mickey had had an explosion of rage during group meeting time. Jean and Jeff discussed this, trying to piece together events in ways that Mickey had experienced them. Mickey had given signals early in the free play that he was anxious and jumpy. Jean was pleased that the assistant teachers, Sue and Bud, had been sensitive to this so that when he was splashing water around at the sink, Sue was right there with sponges and siphons to lead him to the water table. Later on, Jean said:

> When he was painting his costume he was pouring the paint on, and Bud went over and I thought, "Please don't say, 'Stop pouring the paint.'" And Bud said, "Oh, look, you can use the brush to move the paint around," or something like that, so I thought that was good follow-up, too.

The reader cannot hear the depth of concern in these spoken words, but it underscored Jean's strong personal-professional relationship with Mickey. It had a person-to-person, not a teach er-to-pupil, quality. Given a chance to think about the morning, Jeff recalled the beginning of the end for Mickey. He had very much wanted to share Peggy's carpet square at group meeting when the rule was one child, one square.

JEAN: Why couldn't two sit on one carpet square just then?

JEFF: They were too smushed together—so I, um, just asked one to move, and right away Peggy got up, started to move, and also Mickey ran around back, and said, "I'll go sit over there," and then Bud grabbed him and said, "Peggy's going to go over there—sit back down here," and everything seemed fine, but I think that was it.

JEAN: In 2 or 3 minutes, and he had had physical contact with you, being squished in, being put on the other side of the circle. You didn't lift him up, but there was some physical direction there; he got up and Bud took hold of him, and I wonder if all that physical contact, um, might have been uncomfortable for him. I don't know, just a guess—I wonder if the physical adult touching does something for him.

Had her interest been only in the rules of classroom living and management, she would not have hypothesized about Mickey's outburst in ways that would support the meaning to this young boy of being close to Peggy and being touched by adults. After being passed from hand to hand in his numerous foster placements, it is likely that the touching, guiding hands of adults, especially when moving him from a person he liked so much, could at times be felt as intrusive and punishing to this abused child. Refusing to dismiss his behaviors as "unpredictable," Jean engaged in speculation about their sources and their rationality to Mickey as a way of coping. Strategies followed for responding to Mickey with sensitivity, and consciousness was raised about the special meaning he might very well be imputing to touch.

In her work with Mickey, Jean looked for sources in the environment where the rage might be generated that found expression in face slapping and throwing tires at children. She was concerned about his experiences in the special education setting. She said:

The thing that was most striking to us when we went on a visit was that there were three chairs, three child-sized chairs. . . . Mickey was in a chair. The teacher sat in back with her legs around Mickey's chair. Downstairs he sits on a chair like anyone else; he does a collage for 15 minutes.

Seeing Mickey in that situation I can understand that in that intense structure, if someone had me pinned in a chair, I'd probably haul off and start swinging my arms also.

Empathy is fostered by a grasp of the complexity of human behavior. It is not a simple matter of labeling human activity "unpredictable" or "immature." Jean tried to track down the causes for Mickey's behavior, which she did not view as "irrational."

Because of his acting out at home, the other setting was using a reward-and-punishment system that involved the foster parent's giving him happy or angry faces to take to the teachers. Contingent on behavior at home, the child was being rewarded or punished. Jean viewed this as another reason for his anger. First of all, young children struggle with concepts of time; for them, events removed in time are not as easily connected as they are for adults. Second, this strategy treated him as a nonperson. He had no representation at the trial of what was good or what was bad behavior. His reasons were not taken into account, it seemed. There was an assumption of fallibility of the child and infallibility of the foster parents. Jean knew that she was sometimes regarded as critical by the special education setting and that mainstreaming in the nursery school was itself an experiment. She saw a need to go carefully because she was "paving new roadways." But she did share this concern with one of Mickey's teachers who had her own ambivalences and wanted to "find some common ground with Mickey" when the clipboard program was put away, for instance, "when he's taking a bathroom break." Jean recognized that the special education staff acted with the best interests of Mickey in mind, operating from a different value base than hers.

Mickey's world was not a strange, uninhabited place to Jean. She imagined how she would feel in his shoes. It was his third foster home, which he shared with an acting-out, emotionally disturbed girl. The foster parents did not have an easy time, and Jean put herself in their shoes, too. Jean described their disappointment and frustration with the two small children they were raising. One day they were so pleased to have a new sand pit full of clean sand for them. Within no time Mickey and his foster sister emptied it of sand hurled wildly around, some at each other, as they turned the treat into a torment.

Each day he rode a bus with seven other children, older children who attended a school for children with special needs. One boy on the bus engaged in bizarre gesturing and was often teased and provoked into this by the other children. Some days Mickey entered the classroom in a high state of excitation. Jean said, "We don't expect some mystical transformation when he enters the classroom." She tried to be close to him or guide another adult to help him move in to prevent his rushing around dropping tissues in the fish tank, sweeping objects off shelves and tables, and otherwise releasing his distress on his environment.

Early in November, Jean had felt angry with Mickey about a fish tank incident. When her anger cooled she said, "I wanted to be kind and gentle to him again, so I took him on my lap. One day he sat on my lap and I rubbed his leg. I stopped. He took my hand and rubbed it back and forth on his leg." She knew that touch had different meanings for him, at times negative and at other times much valued and enjoyed. Being in tune with her own feelings was characteristic of Jean, and working with Mickey brought her anger and apprehension as well as joy and satisfaction.

Mickey Moves Forward

Jeff finished his placement at the end of the fall semester. In April he went back for a morning's visit and a royal reception by Mickey:

> Yeah. He was making me all that food when I was sitting there, birthday soup with all the things in it. He was washing up and he started washing my shirt [laughter]. He put water on it. I said, "Well, I want to keep this shirt dry—it was clean this morning." So he ran over, got a paper towel, came back, and started to dry me off.

Mickey was still enjoying water play as much as ever, but his imagination was evident, and he seemed to have a new ability to care for a wider circle of children and adults. His own experiences of the consequences of getting clothes messy could be transferred to Jeff's concern, and Mickey acted empathically. In a classroom, where how he felt engaged the teacher's energies, Mickey perhaps found enough energy to enter with empathy the worlds and feelings of others on rare occasions such as this.

Peggy and Mickey throughout the year stayed close friends. Typical of their talk in the fall was the following: "No—I—want—to—stay—here, Mickey" said in her quiet, staccato, slow voice. They frequently played parallel, but they would check to see the other was there and where they sat at group time. This was clearly important to Mickey, and Peggy would be very sad when Mickey was absent until Jean consoled her by letting her know he would be returning. These two needy young people found a source of comfort in each other, always helpful and supporting, each approving of what the other did and made. But as the year advanced, they moved out increasingly to other children, broadening their circle. Peggy's speech became clearer. Mickey continued to be active but often very anxious and very concerned.

An episode at the end of the year illuminated how this group of young children and their teachers responded to Mickey on one of his very worst mornings. But first there is more to know about Marcia, the "belle of every ball," the "mother."

MARCIA

Leaders spring up in groups. Marcia's leadership, it has been noted earlier, was a concern to Jeff because he felt that she was taking initiative from other children whose development might be hampered. Jean was aware of this and responded as will be described. She and Jeff valued Marcia's initiative but were aware of the boundaries they would need to help form if she were not to dominate. These took a variety of forms, which are discussed, following a few illustrations to fill out the picture of Marcia at school.

Jeff caught the typical thrust of Marcia's language in the fall as she played with Johnny. He declared, "We need more soap."

But Marcia protested, "No—we have enough soap right here! Stop getting soap all over me, Johnny! Rinse the table! Just rinse the table! Are you guys rinsing the table? Are you? We don't need any more soap!"

Marcia's Leadership

Through the year the number of commands shrank as Marcia's language reflected her imaginative ability to incorporate others through thinking up enticingly interesting ideas that gave them something to do in their own way and in their own time. This development seemed related to the ways in which Jean and Jeff worked on countless occasions to clue Marcia in to the needs of other children. As adults who were trying to enter the children's worlds, they served as powerful examples for perceptive, sensitive Marcia to both imitate and model.

At group discussion time Marcia presented a problem early in the year because, never at a loss for a comment, she could and did monopolize the conversation. When Jeff was showing the children a flannel board story of the Pilgrims, the *Mayflower* accidentally fell off the board. Marcia laconically concluded, "And they all drowned." Frequently she suggested an end to group discussions, either directly ("This is boring") or indirectly ("How about we get up and play?") or sometimes bidding for sympathy ("Is it time to get up yet? My feet are falling asleep"). In the latter instance, Jean acknowledged Marcia's feelings but was not ruled by them when she quietly told her, as reported earlier, "Wiggle them, Marcia." Jean continued the discussion for a brief while only because, in fact, Marcia was often an accurate barometer that recorded when group interest had dropped and fidgeting levels had risen to the unbearable.

She enjoyed helping Jean, and she was interested in virtually every activity offered. She was flexible when her overtures were rejected, which happened, even in November, as children found their own initiatives, as Robin did in the dialogue below:

MARCIA: [bossily] Come on, we're going on a date somewhere. We're going on—a—date.

[Robin ignores her.]

MARCIA: [in a sweeter voice] Wanna play house with me?

ROBIN: [very flatly] No.

MARCIA: [confidentially to Margaret] I may have to go out to dinner by myself . . . with the baby [as an afterthought that seems to strike her as a nice idea].

She, Robin, and Johnny had the basic advantage of being old-timers, which gave them an edge as leaders. Marcia's advantage was enhanced by her freely flowing language abilities and her zest. She was never without someone ready and willing to play with her because she was talented at thinking of play themes and of ways of incorporating other children into the play. Brad, the smallest, youngest member, was frequently included in her play, and throughout the year she was often found making a place for him, as she did in the following incident recorded in November. Jeff had asked the children in the block area, which included Marcia, if they would like help. Marcia responded, "We don't want any help. We're doing just fine!" as the rest chorused: "No help! No help!"

Assistant teacher Bud, asked Brad if he would like to build his own house because Brad was standing looking rather forlorn on the sidelines. A chorus of voices chanted, "No help, no help," but Marcia made a place for Brad, and he was included by the others.

Later in the morning Brad, talking to Marcia in a very whiny tone of voice, received a sharp rebuke, "Brad . . . stop acting like a baby," followed by a much kinder remark, "You're GI Joe, right?" which pleased Brad.

In December, Jeff reflected on his teaching in relation to this strong young girl and the needs of the other children. The reader may recall that Jean had supported him in observing what her leadership meant to Marcia and the group. Jeff wrote:

Marcia's spontaneity often is specifically positive for other children or the group as a whole. Often, Marcia will verbalize things that are happening which would not otherwise be brought out. For instance, one day she said to Mickey, who was painting his Halloween costume, "Boy, you're gonna have a fun costume for the party, Mickey." The look on his face seemed to show that Marcia had helped him make the connection between his artwork and a class activity. On another occasion, the class visited the psychology testing room early in the year, and all were very apprehensive. Marcia broke the ice by starting to yell, "Where is it? I can't see!" when unable to view the task the testers were demonstrating. This loosened up the class considerably, and children and adults alike owed the lessened tension to Marcia's forwardness.

Jeff began by feeling a sense of concern for Marcia's domination, but, like Jean, he later began to expand his own interpretation of events to include meanings they might have for the children. Much of Marcia's leadership was helpful. Much of her conversation stimulated ideas that Jean and Jeff were able to build upon and extend. The trip to the fire station that followed the discussion recorded below was given added significance because Marcia raised certain concerns, thus stimulating some of the other children to share their information and misinformation.

In February, during free play, Marcia was holding forth in great detail on what one should do if one caught fire or if there were a fire in one's bedroom. Simon was full of misinformation. Marcia tried to clarify his ideas, and she told him that you should roll on the floor if you caught on fire, his answer being to "put water on it." Marcia rolled around on the floor saying she would cover her face with her hands. Jean was listening to this conversation; she fed into it by asking what they would do if they were in a room and the door felt hot.

MARCIA: You *must* feel the door. If it's hot, don't open it.

SIMON: If there's smoke coming out there . . . ?

MARCIA: I'm going out a different door.

SIMON: Cover the crack. . . . If you smell the smoke, you could kinda cough.

MARCIA: [as if reciting a formula] Never—hide—from—a—fire because a fire—will—find—you.

Three-year-old Brad, who had been on the fringe of this, came over to me and looking soberly into my eyes commented, "If you want a healthy baby, don't smoke."

Following this discussion, the children went to a group

meeting. They were interested in the peanuts and water that they saw in the center of the circle. At one point, several children were talking at once about "their" brands of peanut butter. Marcia chastised them for talking at the same time.

MARCIA: Take turns, everyone. Raise your hands.

JEAN: [raising her hand] I have something to say.

MARCIA: [smiling knowingly] The *teacher* isn't supposed to raise *her* hand.

JEAN: [quietly] How will you know I have something to say if I don't raise my hand?

CHILDREN
IN CHORUS: You'll say it! You'll say it!

Marcia Learns

Marcia articulated the rules and the children obeyed. The conversation veered back to fire and its hazards, and Marcia called out without raising her hand, "Little boys and girls shouldn't touch a stove without a pad." Simon in his gentle way reminded her that she had not raised her hand. Hoist on her own petard, she giggled. Marcia had begun by educating the group, but the group ended by educating her in the enactment of this rule. Jean, quietly observing, demonstrated her belief that children can learn from each other and noted carefully what she needed to draw to their attention, not necessarily at that moment. (Later she expressed chagrin that the children had conceptualized the role of the teacher in such a stereotypic way. They were not called upon to raise their hands in her class. We speculated that the media and their families and communities had built a powerful image of what a teacher should be that held its own despite the firsthand experiences of the classroom, which differed significantly from the image.)

Jean's belief that children can act as teachers as well as learners had found enactment in this incident in which Marcia was taught by Simon. Jean spent much of the morning listening to and talking with children at their level physically, frequently in one-to-one conversations that I could not record because they were person-to-person, not TV-commentator in style, audible to all and impersonal. Her expression of concentration and interest seemed evidence of her belief that young children have much valid, interesting knowledge and that it was part of her work to see that this knowledge found a place in the educational program.

Jean did not want Marcia to dominate, but she did not want to extinguish her leadership. Balancing this girl's drive and initiative with other children's needs was a thrust in Jean's teaching. In the following example, Jean gave Marcia some lessons in constructive leadership. There is evidence later in the chapter that the lesson was learned.

Marcia loved playing teacher. In the following episode Jean supported her in this. It was late April, and Marcia had told Jean she wanted to teach the children how to make a book. Jean agreed and asked Marcia what preparations she needed to make, whereupon Marcia went off to get some paper. Marcia sat in Jean's chair (although Jean usually sat on the floor) and became impatient when the children continued to be busy at their pursuits and were slow to form a circle. Marcia commanded, "Everybody should be sitting."

Jean pointed out that some children were finishing their work, specifying what they were doing and so clueing Marcia in to the world of others. Robin was seething with what looked very much like envy as he watched Marcia become teacher. As they waited for the group to assemble Marcia read the sign *School Crossing* as *Bus Stop*. Robin fumed and in a high-pitched, very cross voice scolded in a deliberate way, "And you're a silly one, 'cause it doesn't spell *bus* anyway. Now!!! [huff-puff noises] *School* does *not* spell *bus*." Marcia paused but was unabashed as she looked at the words and said, "But there's an *s, s*, and *s*." Robin could not believe his ears, but he conceded the hopelessness of continuing the argument, pursed his lips, and remained silently waiting for what came next. Marcia folded the paper in her hand and gave vague instructions for bookmaking. Robin had an inspiration: "I think I know where you got the idea from! From the show 'From These Days.'" Marcia gazed blankly at him. Jean had been taping the group talk, and she played it back to them. Everyone, especially Robin, dissolved into laughter. Marcia had had her two or three minutes of being teacher. Jean had no intention of letting her keep the group captive, so she directed those children who wanted to make books with Marcia to go to the end table. Robin, Pat, and Johnny went with her, but all four stayed only a few minutes; then they pursued other activities.

In the bookmaking lesson, Marcia used her initiative, supported and guided in this by Jean, who pointed out to her that other children had work to do. The other children had learned to hear Marcia's good ideas but not to be absorbed by them so that their own initiative was stifled.

Sharing Initiative

Earlier in the morning of this observation, Marcia had interacted with Simon, using her initiative but not at the expense of Simon's. All the children were invited to Simon's birthday party. It was free play period, and Simon and Marcia paired up. She told him, "We're still girlfriend and boyfriend" (yesterday she had married Kevin). Simon asked cheerfully, hopefully, "Are we going to get married or what?" as they whirled around the floor. It was a small classroom, and Marcia and Simon's whirls had to be stopped because they imperiled block buildings and themselves. They were moved over to the easels (after a search for the calendar), where for the next 20 minutes Simon and Marcia painted side by side, Marcia talking the whole time, making free with suggestions for the painting Simon was working on. Each started with a rectangle, a shape Simon had been exploring earlier; then they diverged, Simon ignoring her suggestions. At the conclusion of making her vivid Mondrian-like painting Marcia did what every teacher of young children learns is inevitable, as she said, "Do you know what's fun?" There was a slight pause. "Covering it!" And cover it with paint she did. Simon did not: After starting the way she had, he had taken his own turn in the path.

The children learned to reject her suggestions without rejecting her, as illustrated in the following incident, which Jean and I discussed late in April.

JEAN: Robin was cutting shapes and bringing them over to me, but I [laughs] I got frustrated. He was bringing me shapes every three seconds, and I told him to take them to Marcia and see if she could use them, and she did.

MARGARET: And she did! She incorporated them in her work.

JEAN: She said, "Oh! Look at these nice little dots I'm making. Simon, you can make nice little dots." And Simon said, "No. I don't want to make dots." [laughter]

We laughed together about this because inventive, talkative Marcia was as free with her suggestions as ever, but the other children now took these as they felt the need, freely rejecting them in ways that brought no discomfort to her. For her own continuing, healthy development, Marcia did not need to be surrounded by followers. She wanted a hearing. She was a very social, lively person, taken with human relationships, marriages and motherhood especially, and with social events, always ready to plan and engage in a party. These urges did not need stifling so much as channeling into ways that enabled Marcia to "take turns." This was not done automatically or by mouthing at her ritual chants, adult "taking turns." Jean demonstrated this in her own behavior by taking her own turn, not monopolizing the linguistic and decision-making worlds of the classroom.

Marcia remained a leader to the end of the semester, but it became a leadership that did not rob others of their initiative. In the following episode she and Mickey played out a morning together in ways that revealed his abiding need to find order and peace in his difficult life situation and her capacity to lead supportively in a caring, constructive way in a group characterized by its cohesive warmth.

One Morning in April

It was one of those endlessly gray, sunless cold days early in April about to provide some snow and sleet. This account of Mickey's morning is presented as evidence of the healing power of a healthy group. Too often the different child is rejected, so it was a moving experience to watch the play described below as it unfolded. There was a stillness in the rest of the classroom as children and adults seemed caught up in the drama of the play centering around Mickey. The account that follows is an expansion of the running notes taken.

At 9:00 A.M. Mickey entered, looking as if invisible ants were nipping away at him. He had a suspicious, angry look on his face. His lips were tightly compressed. He moved, as always, very rapidly and jerkily, this morning heading to the science table where he grabbed a prickly seed. He shouted, "I don't want to have feeled that." Spotting Brad in the housekeeping corner, he flew over there.

Whining, "This is my own house. Don't wreck it," he pushed Brad from the crib, which was large enough for a child. Despite Brad's "No! No!" Mickey pulled the screen around the crib, making a small shelter for himself, saying, "These is my bedrooms." But Brad was not ready to abandon his play—or, incidentally but crucially, Mickey, of whom he asked pleasantly but firmly: "Go in my bedroom?" Mickey in a much gentler tone said, "Okay." To the world in general, Mickey announced, "This is my house."

So much had been going on in the room that I was not sure that Jean had observed Mickey enter. But she had, even as she was helping Marcia retrace her steps to give Thumper, the rabbit, some cold water to replace the hot water Marcia was happily preparing to give him.

Jean approached with a cotton sheet in her hand asking, "Can I put a roof on your house?" Recognizing his need for a place of his own, Jean supported this with a prop. Mickey looked at Jean in a puzzled, almost dazed, fashion. "Wha'?" She repeated her question very quietly and gently to him. He looked pleased and helped to make the roof.

Robin had entered the housekeeping corner, a quarter of which was now covered with the sheet, and he asked Jean in his polite, adult way, "Do you think we could have something over here?" He and Brad talked together inaudibly.

Mickey had made a door out of an upturned scale, which was poorly balanced and in the succeeding play was a source of great irritation to him, since it fell over frequently with a clatter. It fell now for the first time. Mickey was distressed, "That was my new home. I breaked that."

Robin's timing was off as he asked Mickey if he could come into his bedroom. He was sharply rejected. "No . . . these . . . some people break my house. This is my new house." Robin, the diplomat, knock-knocked at the pretend door, and Mickey lightened up, telling him, "If you want to, come in."

Marcia, the ever welcome guest, knocked, too, and giggled with anticipation. Mickey with a ghost of a smile told her, "Oh, come in. Don't break my window." Donald followed, and Mickey yelled: "Don't do [you] break my clock."

It was a small space, and there were many children in it now. The scale fell over. Mickey yelled, "Don't you break my house." Jean moved over and sat nearby. Mickey rejected Stuart, who wanted to enter, telling him sharply, "Don't come in. Go something else. Go somethin' else." Marcia asked Mickey if she might use his phone, to which he assented. Very seriously Marcia said on the telephone, "I'm Kay, okay? I'm Kay, okay. I had to call work, I had to call my Da[dd]y."

Jean noticed Stuart was quite unhappy about being left out of the house, so she asked the children if they could make it bigger so that there would be room for him. Jean asked Mickey if that was all right with him. Mickey assented and then climbed into the crib. As if a drama were unfolding, Robin and Pat stood quietly by watching him. The room was unusually quiet this particular morning.

Marcia had two pussy willows that she announced she was tired of holding. Mickey climbed out of the crib and spoke on the telephone, "That was my friend. I was talking to him on the telephone." Brad asked him, "Mickey, you want to come to my birthday?" Mickey looked noncommittal, frowning briefly. Brad, who could be explosive when rebuffed, quietly went about his business, staying in the house and accepting Mickey's response without overt anger. Marcia moved in with a request, "Mickey, I gotta call somebody, okay?" He nodded at the smiling, approving Marcia, who announced, "Mickey, somebody's on the phone for you."

It was as if Brad and Marcia tried to stay with this distressed young boy in their play, to be his friend at a time when he found life hard. Particularly around Marcia, the tightness of his mouth relaxed, and little smiles came and went.

Without asking Mickey's permission, Angela entered his territory. Mickey shouted angrily, "Don't break that" ("that" meaning the bedroom?). "That was a lot of people—get out." This problem with tenses did not veil the message he was giving Angela, who, nevertheless, did not budge. Mickey persisted. Angela was unyielding, so Marcia mediated. Angela could stay but, said Marcia, "We're not having any more people in here. We're getting squashed."

The scale fell over again. Mickey furiously shouted, "I don't like that." Jean very quietly and very slowly counted the children in the house, "Six children in the house." Mickey stammered, "Like in my, my—my house at home." Jean nodded. Mickey squeaked at Angela, "Mother, you can't go in the house." He waved goodbye to Stuart. His rapid darting movements and the increasing shrillness of his voice were indications that Mickey was about to lose control. No moment could have been more opportune for Marcia to inform him, "We've gotta watch some TV in bed."

Mickey was pleased with this calming suggestion, and when Robin asked to come in, he agreed. Robin entered the tented bedroom and in his usual mannerly way said, as if making polite small talk, "Very shady, isn't it Mickey?" Mickey made a villainous ha-ha sound. Pat squeezed in, and the scale fell over once more. Mickey was livid, screeching, "Some people are gonna break the house."

But angry as he was, he was not flailing out or hitting. He was talking out his feelings, perhaps playing with and sorting out some of his needs and making a solution, temporary as it was, to create his own home. Any port in a storm! Robin said in a very appeasing tone of voice: "Everybody can go in ONLY if there's room, all right?" He seemed to recognize and respect Mickey's need to have his house in order. Always ready with a rule, Robin served Mickey's needs well. Marcia once again relieved the tensions of the moment with a query addressed to Mickey. "Want me to make some breakfast?" Mickey approved. Robin quietly said to him, "Mickey, I'm gonna make a TV. Mickey, save my place?" He bustled off in search of a TV and returned with one. Pat was sent off to get a baby, and Marcia commented, "We're getting a baby-sitter." Pat returned with a stuffed elephant just as the sheet roof fell in on the children in Mickey's bedroom. Marcia declaimed in mock horror, "Who broke this?" adding consolingly, "It's okay, Mickey." Jean came over and quietly, as she put the roof back, explained what happened.

Robin announced, "Marcia, there's gonna be a big party to night," which electrified the children. Mickey, however, scolded Pat, "Don't you break the house." He paused, then added, "We can't 'posed to be break the house." His disconnected syntactical structures mirrored the sense of disconnectedness of this small boy. But his play theme revealed a persistence in his continuing to try to find a safe place that, unlike the many foster homes he had experienced, would not be broken.

Mickey asked no one in particular for a piece of paper. Marcia revealed her own plans for him, saying, "We're going out to dinner, remember?" and Robin chipped in, "Mickey, will you take care of the house when we go out?" (Robin was used to being Marcia's "husband.") Mickey looked blank.

The children scattered to get ready for the party, but Marcia had no baby-sitter for the elephant she was holding. She asked Sue, the assistant teacher, who told her she was sorry but she was going out (pretending). Marcia responded, "I'm going the same place," and dumped the elephant baby in the crib. As Kevin approached the house, Mickey called out, "Not you!" Marcia asked Mickey if he would like to give the baby another kiss, once again defusing the situation.

Merry Kevin had put on a fetching sequined cap, telling the world at large, "I wanna be married." Mickey stuck on the refrigerator a drawing he had made on the piece of paper he requested. Robin asked, "Would anyone here like to go to the party?" and in a seeming non sequitur Brad said, "Hi, guys! Later on, I'll be home." (Brad telephoned home and thought about home and mother a great deal that session.) Marcia warned Brad not to miss the party. Mickey answered the telephone—"Is that you, Robin?"—and "wrote" a telephone message. Marcia found herself surrounded by obstacles in the house, unable to get out, and asked, "Mickey, how do you get out of this house?" Jean added, "Marcia doesn't know how to get out of the house. Where's the door?" The delicacy with which Marcia and Jean honored the logic of the play was impressive. It would have been so easy just to push aside one of the objects forming the bedroom enclosure and so rob Mickey of being the problem solver, the decision maker, and the home owner.

Marcia in decisive tones told Kevin, "I'm not playing married with you. I played it too many times. I'm playing it with

Mickey." Kevin looked temporarily set back, but the moment passed as the children spontaneously broke into a song. Mickey sang loudly, clearly, and sweetly. His face changed as he gave one of his joyful smiles.

The party was going to be held outside the house, and Mickey did not want to leave. To smooth his path, Marcia said, "You can make a sign. How about 'No Entrance'?" Having spent about 45 minutes in the play described above, the children then joined Jean, who had called them to group meeting time. When the children left to go to group time, Mickey shook his head, "No." Mickey stayed behind berating an imaginary boy who was "bad" who "sits in the corner." Mickey, alone in his house, sang and talked: "I'm scared. I don't want—" Loudly: "You go to the corner. You bad. You bad boy. B'ass you. B'ass you. B'ass you."

His peer therapists had perhaps helped him clear away some of his distress. Marcia had experienced a transformation from being a somewhat bossy, demanding girl to a responsive, warm young person with leadership abilities of a constructive kind. Jean and Jeff had each set consistent limits on the leadership she exerted but within the framework of searching for its possible impact on the other children valuing her strong sense of initiative, her need for autonomy.

Neither the behavior modifiers in the other education setting nor Jean and her staff wrought either singly or together any miracles in Mickey's life. In the above episode there can be seen a nondestructive working through of his feelings of badness, of rootlessness, his "new home" fantasy and hope, and his ability to both talk with and work with Marcia and Brad, evidence of his social growth. Jean had her options when Mickey entered as "a blizzard." She could have isolated him with the popular "time out" technique, thus depriving Mickey and Marcia of rich learning experiences. Instead, her beliefs in the learning children can do from each other sustained her judgment that in free play, observed and supported by her, such learnings were a likely possibility. Jean's beliefs about the centrality of play have implications for the experiences the children had in the housekeeping and other areas. Jean protected their time to play.

Perhaps because Jean refused to label Mickey, the children followed her example and saw him as a person. The acceptance—

not condonation—that she showed carried over, so that one did not hear, "Look what Mickey's done now!" Without a judgmental and negative view of him, the children brought their own empathic, caring feelings for this troubled child.

A HEALTHY GROUP

There was some further evidence that this classroom group was healthy. They were warm and helpful to newcomers. In February a mother carrying a baby accompanied by a small, red-headed 2-year-old boy came on a visit to the classroom, which the boy would probably attend in September. Initially he wandered around the room:

> Small boy notices his mother has left. Jean holds the sobbing boy trying to comfort him. Marcia comes up and says gently, "Hi! My name's Marcia." Simon says, quite sadly, "I remember when my mommy left." There is a quietness in the room. Robin comes up to him and asks in his formal best kind way, "How old are you?" The small boy leaves Jean and goes to the play corner and tries opening a cupboard door. Robin says, "Could I help you?" Mother returns and the small boy does several whirlwind turns touching everything he can swiftly and then leaves.

This moving out to strangers is surely a sign of group health. The children built comfortable, trusting relationships with the varying students who had placements with the class. Jean frequently stepped out to the viewing room to observe without the classroom "going to pieces." The confidence she had that children could teach children extended to the students' capacities to both learn and teach them and each other. Sometimes she found it very difficult not to intervene, and her beliefs were tested from time to time. Of course, she would never have hesitated to act if there were any danger, but this was not a problem. Her faith in the students seemed to buoy up their confidence, creating a cooperative, warm classroom climate that was sustained when Jean was not there. In the spring, when Jeff substituted, the children welcomed him back warmly, and several gave him crayon drawings or paintings when he left. He was surprised and pleased by this and jokingly attributed the positive changes he saw to their being "back in capable hands." Growth and maturing must be acknowledged as partially contributing factors, but since not all groups cohere in harmony, other factors are salient. The small, countlessly repeated actions of the early childhood educator surely had impact over time.

There is much to learn about how groups of young children function. Recent research on prosocial behavior is generating new interest in the capacities of the young to care for one another, but it is still possible to enter classrooms where young children are together as Isaacs observed, serving as incidental background for each child's isolated activity. With the heavy emphasis on academics, this is not surprising.

One of Jean's strongest beliefs was evidenced in her initial descriptions of the children, which emphasize the social. When asked to give a brief picture of each child, she said, tongue in cheek, "I take it you want to know more than whether they know the alphabet or whether they can tie their shoes." In an era when knowing splintered skills, shapes, colors, and the alphabet have assumed primacy in many settings for young children, Jean viewed cognitive and socioemotional growth in more complex dimensions. Jean thought of the classroom as a small society, so that fostering social development was seen as significant educational activity.

EFFECTIVE TEACHERS

Almy and Genishi (1979) point out, "To some degree, teachers can measure their effectiveness by the changes they see in the behavior of the group. In an atmosphere in which youngsters feel trusted and safe, the usual direction of such shifts is toward more acceptance, more cooperation, and less antagonism" (p. 112). The shifts in Jean's class were in these positive directions, reflected in Marcia's comment to Jean, "*All* our friends aren't here today." *Friends* was her choice of word. This small girl, as usual, caught the essence of her world and broadcast it.

I believe that more classrooms and settings for young children must be based on the values and beliefs operating in Jean's. The obstacles to this occurring are discussed in the next chapter, after which I will move on to promising steps that can be taken to bring such environments into being by giving needed support to the teachers who help create them.

6 Other Values and Beliefs

Jean held values and beliefs about children, teaching, and education that brought about changes in the lives of those in her classroom. Other values and beliefs inform the work of many educators whose views and behaviors are different from Jean's. It seems appropriate at this point to highlight some of these different operational values and beliefs to illuminate some of the choices that are made implicitly or explicitly by teachers and to examine the consequences of those choices. A discussion follows of some of the obstacles to be overcome when the decision is made to implement the values and beliefs that found expression in Jean's work.

During the period when Jean and I were studying her teaching, another study of teaching was reported by Janesick (1982), who spent 6 months observing and interviewing Ken, a sixth-grade teacher. Both Jean and Ken were experienced teachers, and both were judged effective by the educators describing their work. But they did differ significantly in certain key beliefs with consequences for the children they taught. A brief comparison of Jean and Ken is offered below as a means of underscoring the theme of this manuscript: that values and beliefs, whether implicit or explicit, are greatly influential in the education of children and that conscious choices are the hallmark of the professional practitioner.

JEAN AND KEN

Ken had taught for 10 years, 2 years longer than Jean, in a public school setting. They taught children at different developmental levels, but they shared a common goal of wanting to educate children so that they helped to build their sense of self-esteem and develop their individual talents. Both teachers had a high level of commitment to the children they taught, a concern for their lives in and out of school, as well as a positive sense and conceptualized images of themselves as teachers. Ken taught 30 inner-city children with one aide and one part-time student teacher. Jean's largely middle-class group had a wide developmental range that, as the reader knows, included two children who were mainstreamed. Besides this group, she taught 42 other children she met at other sessions during the week. Both Ken and Jean had taxing responsibilities, which they met with a sense of responsibility and energy, and their children responded positively to this. Ken wrote plays for his class and rehearsed and directed them, using his imagination and initiative, as Jean did when she designed and brought in original materials and created rich experiences. When they were not teaching, it was clear that teaching was often on their minds, because it was much more than "just a job" for both of them.

Beliefs About Children

Both Ken and Jean cared for the children they taught, recognizing that they were like themselves: feeling, thinking beings. Both teachers expressed concern about the children's feelings as well as their cognitive and social lives. Ken said:

> . . . my head isn't only tied up with academic subject areas, and I like to hear about their personal lives and hear about things that interest them, and I want to know about their feelings and let them know I share common feelings. (Janesick, 1982, p. 176)

He took a 10-week training program in learning to lead *The Magic Circle*, a programmed curriculum related to feelings, which was evidence of the seriousness of his commitment. But for Ken the children seemed to be divided into parts to be dealt with sequentially and separately. When the children in his class were upset, he concentrated first on working with their emotions and then on moving to the academics. Jean saw children holistically. She did not believe in compartmentalization; for her, cognitive learning was often charged with emotional significance. This led her to recognize Simon's concern about himself when he tore his silhouette, at the same time she gave him the tape to fix it. With the "third ear" she heard the message in his Humpty Dumpty refrain. With her instructional eye she saw him working on part-whole relationships, as well as on how to solve what is both a psychological and construction problem of putting back together what is accidentally torn apart.

This separating out of feelings and dealing with them in isolation in the curriculum may have accounted for Ken's lack of empathy with the angry resentfulness his class showed when he left them for a brief period of 6 weeks to work as a helping teacher. Prior to leaving them he told the class he was confident they could work together as a class whether he was there or not. In fact, these preadolescent, inner-city children felt deserted, and they went to pieces without him, misbehaving with the substitute teacher and acting out in the library.

Minuchin (1977) points out that the difficulty of having a set curriculum for feelings is that emerging feelings generated by classroom life may be shortchanged. Jean worked with feelings as they occurred in the flow of the educational program as well as having occasional discussions and books about feelings.

Knowledge

Because Jean viewed the children as competent and knowing, she expected them to share in the teaching-learning process, whereas Ken seemed to see the children as lacking in valid knowledge, leaving himself as the bearer and conveyor of knowledge he defined as worthwhile in the classroom. The heavy burden of such teaching fell solely on his shoulders, depriving him in all likelihood of gaining support and renewal from other members of the classroom. In such situations most would experience "burnout."

Perspectives on Teaching

Another difference between Ken and Jean had to do with how they shared their power. Ken planned for everyone, in contrast to Jean's process of letting adults and children make decisions—sometimes a very slow process, but it did make them independent of her presence. Consequently, when Jean left the room and remained out of class for several days, things did not fall apart. When Jeff acted as lead teacher during the fall, Jean was frequently out of the classroom. Leadership was diffused among the adults in the open-system classroom, where adults consulted frequently with each other on the fly and children shared certain aspects of this delegated power.

Jean's view of the teacher as one who orchestrated the team contrasts with Ken's tongue-in-cheek description of himself as a "benevolent dictator." Dependency on him seemed to have been fostered in his sixth-graders, whom one might have expected, as he did, to cope with things without his being there all the time. Jean's 4- and 5-year-olds, at a stage when they are indeed dependent on the adults in their lives, although benefiting in many ways when Jean was with them, continued to learn productively in her absence. In Ken's absence, the children floundered, dependent on the presence of the leader to arrive at positive decisions, which led Ken to question his relationship with the children. Not wholly committed to the image of himself as controller, and searching to make sense of his teaching, Ken speculated, "If they could not cope in a 6-week situation, maybe I was not that good for them in that I was just too much of a crutch and not that good of a teacher" (Janesick, 1982, p. 172). He seemed aware of the dependency he was fostering as classroom power remained in his hands, but there was no evidence that the school as a system provided him with a structure in which to think through his ideas.

As part of his role, Ken dispensed rewards and punishment. Using his personal relationship to guide their moral growth, he asked his children to behave themselves in the library in order to show him that they could have a good library period. This contrasted with Jean's approach, which is reflected in these comments to Jeff. She was pointing out an aspect of his teaching she observed, relating it to her preference not to have children come to adults for praise. She said:

> I noticed that Lee had a scarf tied around her, and she worked
> real hard and you were just going to send Sue over to help

her . . . and she got it off by herself, and you acknowledged
this. You didn't say, "Oh, good job!" You said, "You got it
off by yourself," in a pleasant and not overly dramatic or
condescending voice like, "Oh! Oh!" but acknowledging her
for an accomplishment she made.

Jean's was not a classroom in which children were encouraged to do things to please the teacher: "Clean up for Mrs. Smith,"
or "Be quiet for Mr. Henry." She was there to support them in
their effort, but she regards praise as too often a heady way of
teaching children to obey and please adults mindlessly with
negative outcomes Kamii (1984) has described. Her teaching aimed
to support the children to think through their own decisions and
to evaluate them themselves with the guidance of others in the
room, including herself.

She was very careful not to pigeonhole herself as a teacher,
trying to avoid being a delimited role enacter. When Jean and
Jeff discussed his plans for telling the children about his life as
a pizza chef, Jean expressed her concern that the children understand roles not as separate isolated fragments of the self but
as the varied, flexible, responsive parts of what remained very
much an integrated, consistent person. As she put it, "So when
their dad goes off to work, he's still their dad." She worried how
to put this complex business of roles to the children:

Well, he's not a teacher, now he's a chef. . . . Or, when
you're here you're a teacher so therefore you're not a
chef . . . well, no, you're still a chef, but—this is what you're
doing at this particular time. . . . [laughter] Chef Jeff!

She struggled to establish that the person was the core, a consistent self, responding flexibly to different expectations but remaining a person.

Ken seemed to be struggling with himself as a fragmented,
compartmentalized set of roles. He spoke of wanting to be seen
as human and so "acting goofy" sometimes, and of wanting to
be "father and mother" (Janesick, 1982, p. 184) to some of his
children. Drenched as the literature is with the role model concept, he had perhaps been taught to be distanced from simply
being himself. Jean seemed very much herself when she taught,

not the Jean the teacher or Jean the parent role model. Her voice and facial expressions, whether she was addressing children or adults, were consistently Jean. She did not have a teacher voice. Perhaps because she was not locked in a role, she did not conceive of stepping out of it to be human.

Views of the Educational Program

Just as she did not compartmentalize feelings into a segment of the curriculum, she did not divide the program into work and play, rewards and punishment, or academics and frills. In this holistic approach she was supported by her supervisor and most of the parents. Ken's class was brought into a cohesive whole as they worked under his dynamic leadership in a variety of projects to balance off the "academic" work, but there is no indication that he viewed such projects as rich in potential for infusing rigorous academic learning. In many elementary schools, Ken would receive a little support for viewing his plays as serious, academically honest work. Indeed, Ken felt that he received little support at all from his supervisor in relation to his teaching. Many schools reward a narrowly defined teacher role as dispenser of skills, which Ken tried to go beyond on his own initiative.

Both teachers were constrained in many ways by the systems in which they worked. Both responded to limitations in ways that reflected their active commitment to doing the best for the children they taught. How they conceptualized "the best" seems strongly connected with values and beliefs, which in turn influenced their learning environment and the learners, including the teachers.

Summing Up Jean's Effectiveness

In thinking about Jean as an effective teacher of young children who supported the other adults in their lives it seemed that her values and beliefs acted as guides to her teaching. She refused to break children or education up into small fragments and to deal with them piecemeal. Holistic perspectives of the person and of the objectives of education played a strong part in her thinking. Feelings and cognitions did not come in separate streams but merged, and, although some separation might occur, she felt it was important to keep focused on their connectedness. Basic skills acquisition was valued in the context of present and future substantive learning in the disciplines and the meaning the person imparted to it, which contributed to the fund of knowledge.

Viewing human beings as generators as well as consumers of knowledge encouraged her to create a setting in which all experienced some autonomy and some initiative for the good of the individual, the group, and ultimately of the society because she envisioned the small events of the classroom as contributions to the larger workings of a democratic society.

Characteristically and perhaps most significantly, Jean brought all of herself to the work—an essential feature of being a human service professional. Although much technological expertise is drawn upon by such human service professionals, they also draw deeply upon the persons they are, overcoming numerous obstacles in doing so.

OBSTACLES

Some professionals bring themselves wholeheartedly to their work. Others become fragmented into role playing, distanced from those they want to serve. Professionals can lose empathic perspective of their clients. Without support for their own full personal-professional development a walling off from clients can occur. In a research study (Adams, 1982) of 20 elementary and 20 secondary school teachers covering a 6-year period, the author concluded that as their teaching experience grew, their concern with themselves as teachers declined, but they tended to see an increase in problems with parents, children, and administration. The distancing reflected in this study is two-directional: away from self and away from others.

Distancing

Unfortunately, professional preparation seems to reinforce this distancing. Bucher and Stelling (1977) carried out a study with psychiatrists in training, in which they recorded the changes in their subjects' behavior and beliefs as the training progressed.

They found that, initially, when patients experienced problems, the students, perhaps empathic with the clients, criticized the medical personnel and the hospital. As their training advanced, they became far less likely to find fault in the institution or their fellow professionals and much more likely to criticize the patients.

Responding to a concern about a lack of compassion of doctors toward patients, *Physicians for the Twenty-first Century* (Gen. Prof. Ed. Panel, 1984) reports criticism of the heavier emphasis on transmitting facts than on values that foster caring and concern for patients in the preparation of physicians. Very specifically, the report recommends that the general professional preparation of physicians ought to respond to the developmental interdependence of the whole person as well as the specialized professional, a recommendation that seems just as applicable to teachers' professional development. How the teacher feels and what the teacher believes needs to be a valued component of any program of professional preparation, but this is not always so.

One major thrust in the supervision literature reflects a behavioristic perspective, favoring discussion only of what is directly and reliably observable, overlooking the values matrix of intentions, feelings, and thoughts. By staying on the surface of teaching, complex human exchanges can be lost when the professional, acting as an efficient technician, deals only with the data of the senses. There seems to be a tendency to do this in some clinical supervision.

Staying on the Surface

Clinical supervision, focusing on the objective data of the classroom, gives the teacher and supervisor a set of nonjudgmental protocols. When both bring their own perspectives, the potential for intelligent discussion based on classroom observations of teaching does exist. However, when surface observables are the sole focus, they can be meager food for professional development. In the following summary of a conference reported in a book on clinical supervision (Acheson & Gall, 1980), the first-grade teacher and principal seem to reflect such neglect. The teacher requested that the principal observe the class, described as immature. In the preobservation conference, the teacher commented that when Randall and Ronald chatted and played together, the teacher was unsure how much work was done. The principal asked if they were the only children the teacher wished observed and was told that, since the entire group was immature, all of them should be observed. The teacher's reply to a question about what was meant by immature was standard: Their attention spans were very short, they had not learned to settle down, and they talked without permission. The principal asked if they understood the work set for them, and the teacher said that they did but reiterated that they had a hard time settling down. In particular, Ronald complained or played. The conference concluded with the principal asking the teacher what kinds of behavior should be observed and what categories should be used.

During the observation, the principal recorded surface observables such as who left their seats and how many children were in the room. In the postobservation conference the principal recommended tentatively that Randall and Ronald should be separated and suggested a plan to extend the children's attention span through games.

The principal had taken to heart the view that in clinical supervision "the target" is not the teacher but the teacher's classroom behavior. On target, the focus was on surface observables. Neither principal nor teacher showed an interest in the broad goals of education or the intentions and concerns of the first-graders. The social interactions of Randall and Ronald were curbed without reflection on their meaning to the children. Of course, there are times to separate children, but there is also a need to try to fathom the meaning of children's relationships. Checklists of what children are doing give a slice of classroom life that leaves out their intentions and purposes. Teacher and principal, both acting solely as technicians, simply extinguished behaviors because they interfered with teacher-controlled classroom tasks. The possibilities of modifying teaching or the curriculum were not raised; all changes recommended were to be made upon the pupils by the teacher. It is hard to see what the principal learned in this exchange that might make him respectful of the teacher's practical knowledge. The teacher, by not looking at images and expectations embedded in the label *immature*, missed the chance both of acquiring fresh, less negative perceptions of the children and of reinvigorating the curriculum to meet the children's interests and needs. The intellectual potential of clinical supervision as a time for generating hypotheses lay dormant.

In her relationship with Jeff, Jean tried to use surface observables as important launching pads, because she was most interested in their underpinnings. Jeff talked and Jean listened. Jeff taught and Jean observed. She reserved judgment until she found out what was in his mind, what his intentions were, and she gave him the opportunity to talk about what he had done. One morning Jean was in the observation room with its one-way mirror, but the sound was very poor so that she could see well but heard nothing. During the group meeting, she had observed Marcia say something to Jeff and then stand up and dance. They had agreed that Marcia's leadership did not need adult encouragement, so that Jean was puzzled as to why Jeff let her hold the group captive. But Jeff had his reasons:

> What I wanted to do was try to work in "Ring Around the Rosie" because somebody mentioned it who doesn't usually mention things like that. "Ring Around the Rosie," but I couldn't get that in before Marcia wanted to play "Duck-Duck-Goose." It seemed like, when she said that, the feeling was that she almost had me going. I was like, "Wow!—we should do that." But then I thought, "Wait," and I thought some of the kids would be going along with it, too, and "Duck-Duck-Goose," you know, involves running and . . . it's not an indoor game, and so—that was when I just said, "We'll have to play that when we're outside. Let's go over and make the pictures for Mrs. Thompson."

JEAN: Yeah. You want to take some of their suggestions but not so much that they take control of the day, because although you want to be flexible, and sensitive to individual needs, you still want to feel like—you're the teacher, that's your responsibility to . . .

JEFF: But the song came up and we sang it and then, when Marcia said, "Let's dance," it seemed good to me because the group discussion was . . . gone, I was about ready to end it anyway. So I said that was good and I went right along. So anyone might have thought that I was letting Marcia take over the classroom but I thought that it was okay. . . .

The observables were starting points, not finales. Within the less formal contexts of day care centers and nursery schools, some staff development models are springing up that begin and end with surface observables. For example, in a journal one director writes advice to others who supervise. She says, if there are no problems evident, compliment the teacher and let it go at that. Taking a surface view of teaching, judging by looking, both teacher and supervisor miss the chance to gain a deeper perspective. Director-teacher relationships are not viewed as potential for mutual learning. The teacher is reduced to technician-with-a-problem or technician-in-place. The losses of this distanced relationship ripple through the settings. Environments for children can be optimally educational only when they are also optimal for those who teach them (Katz, 1977; Spodek, 1985).

When teachers find no value placed on their reflections and beliefs, they are not encouraged to pierce the veneer of surface observables in search of deeper meanings. It is safer and probably more rewarding for them to play out the teaching role in a more limited way. The observable enactment of others' expectations becomes central, and the educational setting becomes a place for performing roles. All too easily in institutions, including schools, the role can absorb the person. Instead of serving as helpful boundaries for meeting others' expectations, within which the person has room to be himself or herself, roles can become straitjackets. This process can begin in the early years of childhood.

Role Absorption

Jean-Paul Sartre in his autobiography describes how, at 10 years of age, haunted by fears of death, he saw himself growing old. He and his widowed mother had lived all his life with his stern grandfather, whom Sartre, as a very young child, sought to please by playing out the role of child prodigy set for him by his grandfather's expectations. This role playing removed his trust of himself as a judging, responding person with likes and dislikes. Reflecting on this period of childhood, he says that he felt like a fake. Separated from the fullness of his feelings, his human capacity diminished, Jean-Paul said, "Play-acting robbed me of the world and of human beings. I saw only roles and props" (Sartre, 1964, p. 53).

Many years ago when I was directing the early-elementary school at a Children's Institution, Abbott House, one day 6-year-old Robert asked me in his own words whether he was still a big boy. Relatively new to the institution, he had been the oldest brother in his small, inner-city family. This question disconcerted me, and in the school we tried to reexamine his experiences, asking ourselves in what subtle and overt ways we were treating him and the other children as not "big," in the sense of being competent within their capacities. Robert seemed to feel that we were redefining him as less than big. This self-evaluative question spurred us to look for ways to open up options for him to feel and act big. Children can so easily be locked into limiting roles. They can be rewarded for this sacrifice of themselves, too, as was Sartre.

In the early eighties, I taught a course on supervision in early childhood education. One participant, who had just set up and staffed her own school, told me that one positive outcome of the course had been to find out that as a school director she could continue to be herself. In her advance planning and thinking about the school, she had begun contorting her view of herself to incorporate a "boss" role, she said half-jokingly. This was antithetical to her beliefs and values, but it was the available, dominant mode of functioning of her own experiences of supervision.

The world of work has a plethora of diminishing roles that can rob us of who we are in exchange for what we do. Energies are spent living up to the expectation of significant others whose significance may not have been assessed in terms of our underlying values and beliefs. Viktor Frankl (1963) wrote of this in his account of life in concentration camps. He described the men who fell apart in the camps as those who could not face and endure new life conditions, admittedly of a terrible kind, because who they were had been absorbed by what they did. Their inner resources were so closely bound with their previous role that when the role was taken from them, they crumbled.

This tendency to be swept up by roles has many causes. In an uncertain world, predictability and stability are valued. Playing out one's expected part in an expected way leads to fewer shocks—and fewer surprises, too. When clients become militantly critical of professionals, in self-defense professionals often become adversarial toward those they serve and adhere to rules, regulations, and specific job descriptions fulfilling the role's expectations narrowly defined. Initiative and human responsiveness are put on hold as the role of teacher, nurse, minister, or other human service professional is played out with distance from the clients whether they are children or adults. Role absorption serves as a protective device against fears of criticism and attack. When there is no forum for reflecting on the meaning of our actions and their impact, as professionals we act in isolation, vulnerable and defensive, able to bring only a part of ourselves to their work. And this fragmented self is unlikely to be willing or available to become immersed in the clients' worlds, to see life as they experience it. Feeling vulnerable, it is all we can do to occupy our own cocoon.

Acting as Expert

From a position of safe insulation, it becomes easy to objectify the client. Without the exchange of open, free criticism of our work, it becomes easy to rely on set procedures that acquire their own holy rigidity in time. Such work may have a sense of rightness not to be questioned seriously, and the taste of power that accompanies this is satisfying. Power is not automatically shared willingly or easily in our society. Soberingly, one psychologist notes:

> The greater the degree of power socially sanctioned for a given role, the greater the tendency for the role occupant to exercise and *exploit the power* and for those in a subordinate position to respond by increased submission, dependency, and lack of initiative. (Bronfenbrenner, 1979, p. 92)

This hypothesis acquires additional trenchancy in conjunction with psychological research that provides evidence that certain professions, including medicine, architecture, journalism, psychology, and teaching, are attractive to persons who seek power.

The need to exert power over others comes from many sources, and the emphasis on self in our culture seems to exacerbate competition and oneupmanship. As North Americans, we are proud of achieving but do not enjoy being told we have a high need for power. Since power is often viewed as one person's gain at the expense of another, it is perhaps hopeful that even though we may strive to dominate others, we are ashamed of such needs. But power need not restrict the development of others. Jean Miller (1976) has redefined it to incorporate a connectedness with others even as we feel effective and free, but not at the expense of clients, colleagues, or others. When we arrogate power to ourselves as experts, we add to the anxiety and fear of the surrounding world, a "world in crisis."

The role of expert brings much power in a society that exalts specialized knowledge to the virtual exclusion of other kinds. Kessen (1979) writes of the domination of some experts in the field of child development, noting that they moved into the quicksands of prescription based upon their beliefs and biases, not their research findings. Hapless infants were fed at rigidly scheduled times, and mothers were warned not to play with them. The knowledge of laypersons, including parents, was discounted as these professionals ruled their territory with certainty.

Teachers have found much supervision irrelevant and frustrating; they see themselves as the recipients of the experts' answers to their problems in relationships, often mechanistic and highly controlled, in which one person's knowledge is validated at the expense of denigrating another's.*

MOVING AHEAD

To enable and support others in their search to make sense of life and to contribute to their society, professionals in the human services can choose not to act as authority figures passing down

---

*For example, one expert on supervision observed a lesson on fractions taught using cupcakes. The children became disorderly, focusing more on eating than dividing. Unable to resist advice giving, the supervisor recommended using crackers or apples because "students will enjoy eating them afterward but won't be in such a frenzy of anticipation" (Hunter, 1984, pp. 181–182). This conclusion does not seem too arcane for a teacher to reach, given a quiet moment to reflect.

ideas and knowledge to the client on a one-way street. Knowledge can be viewed as exchangeable in a reciprocal relationship: Clients can be seen as creators of unique knowledge that does not compete with professional expertise but complements and extends it. By sharing power and rejecting the omniscient stance of the expert, teacher educators, teachers, supervisors, and other human service professionals can choose to live with uncertainty, dependent on reflection and collaboration with colleagues and clients. This difficult and uneven approach is worth the effort for the benefits it bestows on clients, the self-renewal it can bring us as professionals, and the hope it inspires of a better society.

To sum up, different values and beliefs inform and influence the work of teachers and other human service professionals. At least a part of these differences may be attributable to professional development programs. In the next chapter, the focus is upon a few ways professional development can and does support the values and beliefs that found enactment in Jean's teaching.

7 Implications for Professional Development

In writing this concluding chapter, I have tried to identify the professional supports needed by Jean, Jeff, myself, and others in the human services who share our values, beliefs, and goals.

We need help in continuing to see our child and adult clients as human beings, actively participating in making the best sense out of life that they can, not as cases, pupils, or objects of study. But the wealth of research and advancing technology can shift us into an objectifying stance. We need to attain complex technical skills in assessment. Such skills can have value, but only if a balance is struck between them and human concern and compassion. Attaining such a balance and then maintaining it is not easy. Despite the best intentions conceivable, it seems likely that most of us can sustain the efforts of this way of working only with help. The renewal and satisfaction that come through working with others are sources of strength, but additional built-in supports are necessary to reduce objectifying and distancing.

It is necessary for us to receive the support that comes from being viewed as active participants in giving meaning to life. We must be seen as generators as well as absorbers of knowledge, with recognition given to the practical knowledge we hold, an amalgam of our experiences and formal and informal studies. When respect is shown for our human capacities, we are less likely to view clients as empty vessels, dependent upon and ultimately draining us.

Embedded in this support are the conditions that enable us to feel a degree of power, autonomy, and ease in taking initiative. These are essential for the healthy development of ourselves as persons and adult learners who continue to grow, not locked into a sterile conception of our role. Essential to all these supports is a structure for exploration and deepening of values and beliefs in a search for ways of implementing them more fully in practice.

In the best of all possible worlds, we would find these supports in schools, hospitals, and other institutional settings, where we would be seen as valuing, contributing, knowledgeable members of the human family, not as role players in organizational dramas. Such institutions do exist, and I will conclude this book with some brief thoughts on the decade I spent working in one of them. Before this, I would like to expand on some of the ways that the supports mentioned earlier are being enacted. My purpose in doing so is to leave the reader with a sense of hope and optimism offered by their presence in the world of work.

A BALANCE OF THE TECHNICAL AND THE HUMAN

That our technologies are running ahead of our wisdom is common knowledge. In early childhood education, there exist today quantities of assessment and evaluation instruments growing out of research. The vast expertise of measurement technology expands to be used well or foolishly. The reader may understand our surprise when Marcia failed the readiness test for entrance to kindergarten. This was painful evidence of the technology of testing running amok, saved, however, by the judgment of a kindergarten teacher who valued Jean and Jeff's longitudinal observations of Marcia as evidence of her ability to learn in a group setting. Nevertheless, Marcia's failure was a sharp reminder of the importance of retaining our heritage of child study, in which children's observed strengths hold a central place, with tests fitted into the context of study of the whole child.

Balanced child study centers on entering the world of children to begin to tap into the meanings they are creating, viewing them as whole persons, not teachable objects. It involves observing children under a variety of conditions, talking with them, listening to them, and viewing their behaviors sympathetically as ways of coping with life with the best repertoire of strategies available to them. It also involves learning more about the worlds that enfold them such as family, community, ethnicity, gender, and race. Ways of gathering such information are described well by Almy and Genishi (1979), Carini (1982), and Cohen and Stern (1978).

This kind of ongoing qualitative child study runs counter to the climate of the times; it is longitudinal and not instant, it is time-consuming and not timesaving, and it increases instead of reducing complexity and uncertainty. Creating a balance, qualitative child study complements the use of data from quantitatively oriented studies so that the norms derived from study of populations need not overshadow or displace the uniqueness and variability of individual persons.

In her setting, Jean found the support that is an outcome of longitudinal, qualitative study of each child. As the data relating to the children's development grew, her hunches about the children and how she could help them were discussed frequently with the students and the parents. Time was allotted to the complex problems of growth and development, so that responses to children were not superficial but grew out of immersion in the children's development.

One consequence of this was that Marcia's initial leadership behaviors were not labeled before they had been observed over time. They were viewed not in isolation but ecologically, with children and teacher interaction and responses noted. Jeff was intrigued with the varied meanings of Marcia's leadership to the classroom occupants. His increasing technical proficiency in observation skills gave him rich data, which brought him closer to Marcia as a person, which in turn contributed to his growing abilities to teach well. Through study of Marcia's behavior as leader, he traced its many positive outcomes, including the timid outsider who was incorporated by her suggestion and the enriched complexity she introduced imaginatively. As he began to respect a leadership he had first seen as needing to be "extinguished" to some extent, he also began to see new paths for his teaching. He became skillful and imaginative himself in his responses, two examples of which are reported below.

In the first example, Marcia had led play involving Oscar the Grouch, in which a small group around her huddled together, shoving away all others. This play seemed to be going on so long that it held the class in thrall. Jeff wrote:

> As I approached, the "Get away!" cry went up, but I
> weathered it and calmly stated that I thought this was the
> ice cream stand and that I wished to buy a hot dog. This

struck their fancy, and the "grouchiness" was discarded, as they began to dispense "ice cream with gravy on it" to the several children who joined them.

In the second example, Marcia had set a rule that only the children in dress-up clothes could join the dancing troupe of which, in her black lace cape and ballet shoes, she was both principal dancer and choreographer. In Jeff's words:

> I also intervened during the only-those-dressed-up-can-dance edict of Marcia. I told Marcia I'd like to dance and was given the same reply as the others. But I persisted, saying, "Sometimes I dress up when I dance, and sometimes I dance without dressing up." Then Marcia agreed, saying, "Okay, everyone can dance."

Jeff had learned to put his observations to work. He had also learned how to enter the play, expanding it in ways that fed the imagination and made new understandings available for the children. Moreover, he gained personal as well as professional satisfaction in these shared experiences with the children, whose purposes and plans he respected. When human and technological aspects overlap, they can provide a newly intensified focus for professionals.

Support for this kind of child study was made available in the New York State Experimental Pre-Kindergarten program, which provided funding for the schooling of economically disadvantaged 4-year-olds in six districts of New York State. The effectiveness of the program was judged quantitatively by pre- and posttests and qualitatively by 5-year longitudinal studies of children.

Through study of children as they went through the early years of schooling, the meanings of the education program in their lives were traced. Teachers had an opportunity to meet in child study seminars to discuss their observations and sometimes to hear in detail about the continuing growth and development of a child they might have taught in prekindergarten who was now in second grade. This funded child study was extended to a number of other districts, and I served as a consultant to one of them. In a group made up of 24 prekindergarten-through-second-grade teachers and the school's early childhood specialist, we met for four afternoons a year to study together one child in each teacher's classroom (Yonemura, 1980).

Routinely, most of the teachers in the group kept folders with representative samples of all of the children's work, including dictated stories and drawings and their own anecdotal records on the children. When time permitted, teachers set aside 5 to 10 minutes to talk with a child one-to-one to get at the child's thinking without putting words in their mouths.

We focused on one child as a way of thinking about all the children, sharing the knowledge of the teachers about them, wondering about the impact of the educational program, and getting perspectives on teaching that worked, and why it did and what other options might have been available. The information gathered and discussed flowed out of the teaching day and took many forms such as children's work, their art, dictated stories, and so forth; memories of incidents that stood out in the day could be jotted down later; once in a while we drew upon an audio- or video-taped session and some notes of a child's activities by a student, colleague, or principal.

Practical Reasoning

In these sessions, we engaged in a process Reid (1979) describes as practical reasoning. It involved appreciation, deliberation, and then judgment as we listened to a teacher talk about a child. Appreciation is time-consuming, so feelings that the talk was rambling did arise. Looking over Seurat's shoulder as he painted the countless dots of his pointillistic masterpiece *Sideshow*, one might have wondered just what all the dots would amount to. As a teacher recounted detailed anecdotes involving a study child, I was not alone in wondering what the small fragments meant. This round-and-round-the-mulberry-bush talk, however, invariably supplied food for thought. Having patiently waited for the pattern to build up, the design became clear to us.

On occasion, one piece of information was enough to build a sense of closeness with a child and family. One teacher shared a drawing her study child had made in school after 4 days of severe winter snows that had virtually immured families in their own homes. This very quiet girl returned to school, unusually vivacious, which her teacher was pleased to see. The morning of her return, the girl made a crayon drawing in which a yellow-and-orange mother held center stage with a large baby at her left and our girl at her right with several small figures under the mother's feet. All the figures touched. The closeness and con-nectedness of the figures and the brightness of the mother sug-gested to the group that, despite their being shut in, the closeness had been satisfying. There was a feeling of empathy for the moth-er with those children under foot. The messages in the painting were inferred and formulated tentatively, not stated as pronounce-ments. But the empathic feelings of all present toward the mother were not tentative, and they served the valuable purpose of creating a feeling of connectedness with the home, something not always easily come by.

During these sessions, the teachers had much to say, draw-ing on the reservoir of observations about the children stored in the back of their minds. Some were initially ill at ease with this teacher talk and looked to me as the consultant to fill silences. It is not only children in our society who are conditioned to the rapid-fire pace of television; most of us find deliberative reflection a new, even unsettling way of approaching professional work. Many teachers have additionally tended to absorb the current devaluing of their practical knowledge.

As a general component of the New York Experimental Pre-Kindergarten child study program, respect for teachers' knowl-edge was built in. Significantly, in the child study seminars, it was strongly urged that the role of chairperson revolve instead of being assigned by hierarchical position or special status in the school. This rotation contributed toward minimizing the domi-nance of one point of view and permitted teachers' voices to be heard (Carini, 1982). Teachers needed time to experience their own empowerment through this approach, because it had not been part of their general experience. In retrospect, I see that I could have been helpful in raising empowerment as a topic for discussion.

In time, most participants became comfortable with the deliberative, reflective mode of these conversations, during which we all worked to make sense of the children's worlds and to enlarge them through the impact of classroom living. Child study of this kind supports professional development in which all participants experience some autonomy, use their initiative and find time and a receptive audience to think through not only what works in practice but why and whether that is the best way, and engage in all this thinking in a climate where children are perceived as human beings, not objects of study.

The sessions gave the teachers a chance to know consciously what they knew almost subconsciously about children. Unless a conscious effort is made, the data in teachers' heads do not get a hearing, the rich patterns that are available do not become visible, and a very rewarding, intellectually stimulating part of teaching is lost.

RESPECT FOR PRACTITIONERS' KNOWLEDGE

In this qualitative child study, the knowledge in teachers' heads finds recognition and validation. This practical knowledge is little understood, and the tendency to view it as intuition has meant that it has been relegated to limbo or disparaged as "wizardry" (Hunter, 1984) as far as most researchers have been concerned. Promisingly, Schon (1983) has made a strong case for rethinking practical knowledge. He has discussed the way professionals think in action, and he proposes that such thought be brought to a level of consciousness that enables it to be studied intellectually. He questions the hegemony of knowledge from the formal disciplines as the only significant source upon which practice relies, practitioners becoming the consumers of research carried out elsewhere. While not denying the validity of knowledge in the disciplines, he makes a case for further exploration of the knowledge that is generated as a part of practice, for an exploration of the thinking underlying how practitioners perform.

This practical knowledge, although devalued, is evidenced on the many occasions when teachers comment on how much they learn from each other on those rare occasions when opportunities to observe each other at work are made available and also at more informal times.

Peer Relations

It is not only teachers who value the knowledge of their peers. The psychiatric interns studied by Bucher and Stelling (1977) reflected the value they placed on their peers in such comments as "The only good thing about an assignment to a state hospital was the discussions held with a peer on the long drive out there" (p. 112), and, "I know when I want to talk a case over with somebody, it's with somebody whose opinion I think something of. Which really is true for all my co-residents, and I respect all of their opinions" (p. 112). It is likely that their practical knowledge, shared feelings, and experiences drew them into a relationship that fostered shared learning.

Teachers centers are a promising response to the need for building and expanding the learning experiences teachers can participate in designing and enacting themselves, incorporating consultants and other resources when they decide that they have a contribution to make. A recognition that peer relations are potentially significant is found, too, in a number of teacher education programs. A brief overview of the experiences of Jean and Jeff and myself in peer teaching-learning seminars is offered to illustrate just one approach to structuring it into a program of professional preparations (Yonemura, 1982).

Jean attended a seminar for experienced teachers and Jeff a seminar for student teachers, both led by me. The purpose of the seminars was to explore the values and beliefs underpinning the participants' own teaching, to bring to awareness the reasons for the strategies and options they used, to make conscious the knowledge stored in their heads, and to connect this with the formal bodies of knowledge available to the profession. Although they represent early gropings toward these ambitious purposes, I will describe the procedures used and a few of the outcomes because I believe they hold promise for supporting us as professionals.

The procedures for the two seminars were basically similar, with the content and my supervisory efforts modified and intended to be responsive to the different experiential levels of the participants. The first step was to begin to reveal the participants' values and beliefs about teaching, children, and education. This was done partially in dyads with each dyad determining who would be the first member studied, for convenience referred to here as *the observed teacher*, with the other member acting as *the observing teacher*. The exploration of values and beliefs took time, but it was an important precursor of the classroom observation by the observing teacher of her peer, the observed teacher. It was the necessary backdrop to understanding in what ways espoused values and beliefs were being put into practice under the exacting conditions of classroom life.

AN EXPLORATION OF VALUES AND BELIEFS

In support of this complex process of revealing a matrix of values and beliefs, sometimes a questionnaire was first administered, followed by a structured interview to guide the conversations (Bloomfield, 1976). The student teachers were asked to write about their classroom as they hoped it would be a year ahead. This gave them a way to express their beliefs and values, voiced as hopes for the future. It also gave the rest of us a way of looking at their present classroom work and their present beliefs in action.

As Jeff looked into his future classroom, he expressed some of his beliefs:

> There is a large part of the day for self-initiated play, during which the children have a great deal of freedom to explore areas they choose through play. I am accepting the children's efforts, emphasizing participation in a wide range of experiences. I enjoy sharing activities with the class and seek to promote an atmosphere in which children are free to grow.
>
> I recognize that if rich, holistic experiences are provided for the children, a broad range of learnings will be encountered. Making pizza, for example, can involve numbers (e.g., how many cups of flour?), scientific principles (baking/mixing), language skills (through talking about their experiences), and social studies (how pizza is made, sold, consumed in the community).
>
> I do not see myself as a fountain of knowledge but rather as a helper in each child's individual learning process.

I seek to foster the social and emotional growth and well-being of the children as well as their cognitive skills. In doing so, I try to give children a balance of freedom and support. My "rules" are not rigid but take into account needs and situations. The things on which I insist are each child's safety and their freedom to reach their highest level of development.

When the observer teacher made a classroom observation of Jeff using nonjudgmental running records, this essay was effective in a different way from a rating sheet in permitting her and Jeff to make tentative assignments about his abilities to put into practice what he believed.

Laying the groundwork for the peer relationship, the seminar had a number of foci. Exploring another person's beliefs involved learning to listen, so active listening skills were practiced. Valuing what was being heard as not just "gabbing about teaching" was another focus. Since teachers' practical knowledge is not often acknowledged by researchers or administrators in education, the teachers in the peer relationships did not automatically start off the semester with a sense that description and assessment of what they did Monday morning or Tuesday afternoon was legitimate content for professional study. A case study of a teacher of English (Elbaz, 1981) conversing with a coresearcher on her teaching was very helpful in validating for them their own practical knowledge. Reacting to this study, one experienced teacher in the seminar commented sadly but with a wry touch, "You know, it's nice to see somebody thinks we know something," and the nonverbal response of the seminar was eloquent. Ronald Blythe's *Akenfield* and Studs Terkel's *American Dream* were suggested reading to further the idea that not only professionals but all of us, including the rural poor in an English farm village as well as the panorama of diverse North Americans interviewed by Terkel, possess a wealth of knowledge.

Trust is not automatic even in peer relationships, although they do not have the implicit threat of a supervisor-subordinate relationship. Early in the semester, some anxieties about being observed surfaced. Many reminisced about the supervisory classroom visitation that began with *the* lesson plan and ended with the negative criticisms and reports of minimal learning so often encountered in conversations, the literature, and research on supervision. Building trust among the participants and between the dyads took time.

One purpose of the seminar was to support a nonjudgmental, open, trusting relationship. The teachers were drawn to Eisner's (1979) concept of teaching as an art one might view holistically, and it was equally compelling to them to find themselves cast in the role of a critic who, in his view, is expected to illuminate teaching, to appreciate what works and what does not, thus expanding understanding of it. I think this concept helped build trust in themselves and in the other seminar members.

The rewards of active listening became evident. As one observing teacher noted, her teacher characteristically raised a question about her teaching, which a little later in the conference she answered for herself. As the semester progressed, the observing teachers tended to become guardians of the observed teachers' initiative, abandoning proclivities to make premature suggestions and give advice. As they experienced the knowledge held by their colleagues, their confidence in their own knowledge seemed more evident. When the classroom observations were made, reflections on what had been learned more than filled the 2- to 3-hour seminars.

Role Expansion

When the teachers met as dyads to analyze the data from the classroom observation, they used them as a launching pad, not a procrustean bed. The raw data provided the teachers with mirrors of their teaching and elicited a wide range of questions. For example, Barbara, a second-grade teacher, discussed with Debbie, her observer teacher and a first-grade teacher in the same school, her efforts to broaden her curriculum to include art, since the art specialist had been excessed, in the manner of surplus goods. Her class had spent an afternoon working as individuals on a teacher-directed theme. The products had been very disappointing to Barbara, who described it as an experiment that failed because she had "nothing to put on her windows." During the conversation, Barbara commented that she herself was hopelessly inadequate in art, being able, at best, to draw stick figures. In response to Debbie's thoughts that the children might learn from each other, she was extremely doubtful.

Some seminar members wondered why Barbara was so concerned with the final product, but a few others saw why that would be important. Lortie (1975) has noted how much emphasis is placed on having a visible product, a mural in the hall or bulletin boards, conjecturing that because so much teaching is invisible, an act of faith, it goes unrecognized. Consequently, validation of one's work is to be found in the presentation of such concrete evidence. Several students wanted Barbara to look more at the learning process, what went on before the final products. There was silence. Seemingly at a dead end, Debbie in a tone of offhand surprise said that she was quite talented in art. When a student asked if she could see herself as a resource for Barbara, she said with some surprise, "Well, I guess I could." The isolation of Debbie and Barbara in terms of their mutually supportive strengths was revealed, and steps to change this were feasible in a school where the principal was open to cooperative ventures. Debbie was able to move out of a straitjacketed concept of her role as a first-grade teacher to assume a consulting role based on her strengths. She realized that she had options she was not taking. That expanded what she could do. Barbara, through Debbie's technical assistance, was able to look past her own anxiety to begin to see the contributions in art made by each of her children. Reflections and conversations often revealed choices. Time for such reflection on choices and options with their underlying values and beliefs is central to becoming and remaining a human service professional.

Looking at teaching very closely but "on the outside" gave the teachers a chance to rethink their role as it was being defined for them and by them. They queried the expectations they were to meet, wondered who set them, and asked whether the only response to them had to be mindless obedience. Teachers commented frequently, "Why didn't I see that before?" Immersed in the invisible stream of teaching, they had been given no time to reflect, so that they were robbed of potential ways of improving their work and probably of reducing some of the stresses they felt. Reflecting together, the dyads had the satisfaction of generating their own insights.

The participants valued the opportunity to talk about their work, so the feelings engendered were often very positive. Hard as it was to listen without intruding one's own teaching, the observer teachers found empathic satisfaction as their partners reflected on episodes of their teaching that had been highpoints but that in the course of classroom life had fallen away from their memories. Artists find great satisfaction in retrospective shows, as do their audiences, and these retrospective memories of teaching brought similar satisfaction to the teachers, who expressed delight at the vividness of the recollections of teaching brought to the surface as they listened to their teacher-partners reminisce.

Just as sculptors return again and again to develop the forms they want—but cannot predefine—so many teachers need to go back to learning experiences to reconstruct them. Artists gain strength from discourse with each other about their works, but the loneliness and isolation of teachers has been well documented by Jersild (1955) and by others since. In nursery schools and day care centers, team teaching staff are not isolated in the same way as many elementary school teachers. But even in informal, small-scale settings, it is often uncommon for teachers to have opportunities to observe each other in a way that permits the observer to stand apart for a while and then to have time built in to reflect on what was observed as a valid part of professional life. Such opportunities are sometimes falsely regarded as "luxuries."

Formal Knowledge

As a seminar leader, I asked the participants to sum up some of their thinking in biweekly logs, to which I responded in writing and in face-to-face conferences. The logs revealed the level of learning occurring in the dyads and the efforts the teachers were making to incorporate theories and research. This extract from Jeff's log is an example of this:

> My conversation with Lucy brought out many interesting points about teaching, something an hour-long discussion between two teachers can hardly avoid doing. We talked about the school climate and how the principal and other teachers influenced us. One of her major concerns was the quality of the "play time" in her class. She often feels un-

sure of whether children are benefitting from the experience, and also wonders what level of "wildness," noise, and so on to "tolerate." Since I have also had some concern regarding the play time in many settings, I was very interested in this. I've also heard this type of concern from others in seminar.

Thinking back, as I invariably do, to my own teaching experiences, I decided that "free play" time there could have been called "work time" just as easily, or "time for self-initiated exploration." Play, of course, was seen there as a major way of learning for young children, a time for them to explore many areas of interest. In thinking about "play"—its definitions—I think I came to a fuller understanding of your concern with people's use of the term *free play*, Margaret. How "free" it is, and what exactly it entails, must be specified.

Whatever free play is called, I feel a crucial part of early childhood curriculum is allowing self-initiated exploration of materials: blocks, paint, water, clay, and so on. But I don't think that children benefit from simply being "cut loose" in a room full of material. On the other hand, I hesitate to make this statement, hearing back-to-basics supporters hollering "right!" and waving lock-step, teacher-proof materials overhead.

I think Dewey (*Experience and Education*) made the point that these two extremes must be reconciled and that a sort of "structured freedom" is the key to fostering development. In practical terms, I think this involves providing an environment which recognizes and nurtures children's interests and needs.

In course work, Jeff had met literature on the school as a social system with boundaries and constraints on teacher expectations and on free play. To discuss these in the context of a classroom in vivo with a peer sharing some of the same concerns and to find oneself learning in this way validated both Jeff and Lucy as sources of knowledge for each other, as both generators and absorbers.

Jean acted as observer teacher to Ann, a teacher of 4-year-olds in another setting. In many ways they resembled each other, so their conversations were lengthy and thoughtful. It might well have been Jean speaking when Ann reflected on the time when she realized that there really was no perfect sequence of skills and steps for learning:

Previous to that I simply had the feeling that maybe I
was the only guy in the whole world that didn't know
[laugh]. I hadn't discovered it yet. And now I don't feel that. I
feel a sense of relief and also a recommitment to helping
figure the curriculum out.

And the values she espouses, Ann said, could be found in
just about any book on progressive education. Consequently, as
Jean put it, "So I went to books on progressive education and,
in subsequent interviews, tried to cue into and sort what Ann
said in such a way that they might provide data associated with
a progressive philosophical base."

The conversations led to a theory-practice mix. Just as Jean
used the children's experiences as entry points to the bodies of
organized knowledge of the disciplines, so in work with Ann she
used their shared experiences to make connections with the professional literature, aided in this by Ann, who shared her human
need to order her experiences within a recognized knowledge
framework. My efforts were to support this linkage between experience and formal and informal knowledge.

The experience in the peer seminars supported Jean and Jeff
in their existing tendencies to make sense of their lives, to reflect
on their values and beliefs, to express their feelings, and to care
for children openly and with compassion. There are many ways
of designing such learning opportunities. They take time and
energy, but they can be defended as invaluable for the professional development of human service professionals.

One of the strongest elements in the peer teaching-learning
relations for me was that I was very clearly cast as a colearner.
I needed to listen to what was being brought for discussion, so
that any proclivities I had toward dominating the seminar were
strongly reduced.

But sharing power is not easy. The first time I led the semi
nar, I felt very anxious. I enjoy planning ahead and rehearsing
at length learning experiences that might occur, in broad, not
specific, ways. I had enjoyed the sense of control this brought.
But in these seminars the students were the sources of data; they
set the content. My work came after, not before, the seminar session. It was a shift for me as a teacher. I think coming to understand my feelings of loss and inadequacy in terms of the power

relinquished to be shared with the students was very important for my development. It freed me to listen more openly without the intrusion of too many anxious, self-protecting thoughts.

Professional development was a process in which I was a part. When I planned this book the last chapter was going to address the professional development of teachers. A we-they dichotomy insidiously connected me to a body of literature in which teachers are developed by others. On reflection, I realized that professional development, based on values espoused in this book, involves all or none. Supervisors, aides, teachers, directors, consultants, and teacher educators are joined in an enterprise that must move beyond superior-subordinate relationships in which some are empowered at the expense of others (Yonemura, 1977). Both personal and professional development are contingent upon opportunities to act autonomously and to use initiative, not to be directed and managed as pawns.

SHARED POWER

Even when the work life militates against using initiative, healthy assertive adults try to find a way of stamping their purposes on it. Ronald Blythe, in his book *Akenfield* (1969), which takes its name from his pseudonym for a rural English village, writes of his conversation with John Grout, a plowman of 88 years, who recalls the value formerly placed on precise, exact plowing, although this did not influence the crop in any way. Some farmers would give their plowman free rent for meticulous plowing. As Mr. Grout puts it, "The men worked perfectly to get this, but they also worked perfectly because it was *their* work. It belonged to them. It was theirs" (p. 58). This harks back to the earliest levels of human development, to the basic human need that finds expression in the words of the assertive 2-year-old who resists having his jacket buttoned and declares, "I do it." Professional development needs to be designed and enacted so that we can bring this surge of autonomy and initiative to our own work. The stamp of our uniqueness must be honored if we are not to be technicians only carrying out or supervising packaged educational programs.

Jean wanted children to be reflective decision makers, experiencing autonomy and using initiative. She believed their decision making to be an important, energizing source for her teaching, and she wanted Jeff and the other assistant teachers to understand this, too. For the sake of the children's perception of power allocation in the room and for the sake of the assistant teachers, Jean's supervisory authority was based on shared power.

As a supervisor, Jean did oversee the classroom; she held firm expectations for punctuality, report writing, preparation of materials, and such other behavior needed for the education program to run well. She was aware of her own expertise, but she tried to fit it into the complementary domains of those she supervised. She rejected the role of knowing expert with the ever-ready answer that deprives the supervisees of finding theirs.

She worked toward helping the student teachers increase their knowledge of themselves, repeatedly saying, 'I don't want clones.'' Their own needs, their own beliefs, and their own expectations made them unique, but these needed to be brought to consciousness and to be judged in terms of their impact on their lives and the lives of those they served. In her supervision, then, values and beliefs were the frameworks within which techniques were considered.

As professionals reflect with knowledgeable critics about their work, values and beliefs emerge, so that techniques, expectations, and routines have a context in which to be discussed. In our respective supervisory relationships, Jeff, Jean, and I learned from each other, ventilated our frustrations to each other, and once in a while felt very exhilarated at a shared vision or a new perspective. Supervision can be educative for all its participants when each is viewed as having knowledge and no one claims to have the answers to complex professional problems.

I will conclude by briefly discussing one of my experiences, selected because it represents institutionally structured, programmatically incorporated supports, as distinguished from the more informal, collegial help and guidance that it has been my privilege to find in all my work experiences.

ABBOTT HOUSE

First, as a teacher and then as a director of the early-elementary school at the Children's Institution, Abbott House, I found myself working within a framework of support. Funded partially by the

New York City Department of Welfare and partially by private funds, the institution served about 100 children, 40 of whom attended the early-elementary school set up in a small carriage house in the woods that surrounded the large red brick building where the children lived. I had worked in England in a children's home, so I was prepared to see the school as an oasis from the sterility of group life in an institution. That institutional life here was not sterile was largely due to the philosophy and vision of the executive director, Joseph Gavrin, a psychiatric social worker, philosopher, and poet. His commitment to children as persons found expression in small and large ways. For example, it is both economical and time-efficient to buy clothes and shoes for 100 children wholesale. It is in keeping with a bottom-line view of life. But the children would then have missed out on the experience of trying on, selecting, feeling special, seeing the economy at work, and countless other lessons. Through an effort on the part of all staff, each child went in a small group with two or three other children and an adult on a shopping trip for clothes. In this small way, each child felt special, so it was worth the time and juggling to drive the four miles to the shopping center. We were such good customers at the local stores that the shoe store provided the school with a heavy iron foot measure, which was used frequently in the block corner, where the children built and played shoe store.

The children came and went as foster homes opened up or their families were reconstituted, creating a flux that did not give a sense of stability or calm. Some of the children were physically and emotionally hurt; their rages were understood but were nevertheless hard to live with. We all needed help to remain aware of and sensitive to the children. One support for this took place on Friday morning each week, when regular child study sessions were held. Despite many competing demands, the executive director regarded this not as a luxury but as a priority for everyone, so he always attended along with the program director, counselors who rotated, a consulting psychiatrist, a psychologist, nurse, social workers, and a rotating teacher and myself. We all came with our different perspectives on the one or two children who were to be discussed following brief reviews of newly admitted children.

These different perspectives were respected. No one sat at anyone's feet, hearing the expert give answers. Both the psychologist and the psychiatrist offered illuminating interpretations of behavior that puzzled or irritated or concerned us, but they did not move on from there to prescribe. The team developed a respect for practical knowledge, recognizing that the teachers and the counselors had their own ways of working with children and their own theories of practice. Mr. Gavrin chaired these meetings, but, over time, trust was built that he was not using his position to exert power but to see that the values and beliefs about children we all espoused were finding enactment.

Abbott House was not a paradise of human relations. We were invested in the children, so feelings ran high if someone felt a policy, strategy, or interaction was against the best interests of a child. In the inevitable complexities of the work, we all made mistakes or fell short in some way. The executive director enacted an important value in his response to this: no one was blamed, because he viewed blaming as a block to understanding and clearing the hurdles. Lengthy as the discussions were, they substituted for blame and punishment. Their focus was upon the meaning of events to us, on the values and beliefs beneath them. Some of these distressing times did not get smoothed out—as in any setting—but the underlying values were not jeopardized, either.

These child study sessions were not crisp, businesslike events. At times they resonated with passionate debate, and at other times they rambled round-and-round-the-mulberry-bush until a broader understanding emerged, leaving the group with a sense of high satisfaction. This model of interdisciplinary functioning, in which the status and hierarchy of the professions were not dominant, is one I carry in my head.*

---

*In the Friday afternoon meetings of the advisors in the graduate faculty at Bank Street College of Education, the same set of values was evident. These meetings were devoted to understanding the students we taught, and a psychiatrist and group dynamics specialist served as consultants, eschewing the role of experts. Faculty were not ranked traditionally but as peers; hence the term *advisor* was used, not *assistant* or *associate professor* or *professor*.

The structure of hierarchy dissolved, since all of us were valued participants in the learning process. No one denied the competency and worth of highly specialized technical knowledge, but its worth was viewed as intimately contingent on a balance with human knowledge. These sessions involved us fully as human beings, not as actors at just another meeting.

Such sharing of power and recognition of the validity of others' knowledge, without in any way belittling one's own, contributed to a climate of openness. Because we were minimally self-defensive, our energies were freed to be directed where we wanted them to go: to serve the children. And the discussions did help to do that. I always left the child study sessions with broader views of the children we had thought about and renewed respect for my colleagues. One interesting outcome was that the child whose problems had loomed so large on Friday seemed to be much more approachable and far less of "a problem" in school on Monday morning. Our joined perspectives in the group gave us new individual visions and new energy. No one had given 10 handy tips on what to do with Jason in school on Monday, nor did we need to go in and have him sign a contract to change. I believe that the deliberation and reflection changed us and that our attitude was conveyed to Jason, bringing about no rapid-fire changes but opening the door gently for him to work and play more comfortably.

Time was also built into the work week for professional development activities and for regular one-on-one conferences as well as small-group meetings. These took effort and energy, too, not least because all these sessions demanded written records. All staff were expected to write records on the children, on themselves as self-evaluations, and on the educational and group life programs. These records gave needed structure to the reflective conversations, seedbeds for pearls that were often revealed more clearly and more widely shared when we read each other's reports. Because the setting was so respectful of our different kinds of experience and knowledge, I think it supported me in what I was learning formally in graduate study: that young children were hard at work constructing their workday, that their experiences were valid, and that it was the task of the school to support and extend their knowledge. Rich or poor, children are bent on learning.

Tillie Olsen has described how in the hot July summer of the Depression years, children would play on the slag dumps of a large midwestern city. Although labeled as school failures, "dummies," these children created dramas and acted them; they measured, planned, designed costumes and scenery, and in many ways proved how inventive and clever they were even when their energies were drained by having to look after younger brothers and sisters and carry out chores. These children struggled unaided to make sense of their world, to recreate personal experiences as private knowledge and reconstruct it symbolically. The tragedy there was that they lacked the guidance of caring, knowledgeable teachers who could connect these personal explorations with the formal bodies of organized knowledge, to echo John Dewey.

Children do have to find out early that school has to do with making the world more understandable to them—that they personally benefit from knowing how to read directions and how to read literature, how to compute and how to appreciate elegant solutions, to begin to feel themselves rooted in their history, to know their environment, the geography, politics, economics, and so on. To lose sight of this is to trivialize early childhood education and to reduce it to a time when children acquire only basic skills. Important as these are, they are only a part of a whole set of deep learning experiences that influence substantially what young children will bring to their studies in junior high, in high school, and beyond (Wann, Dorn, & Liddle, 1962).

I feel fortunate to have begun my professional life in a setting in which values and beliefs were central, where my values and beliefs were of interest and concern to my colleagues, where the persons we served were viewed as full human beings, and where all of us were seen as endowed with knowledge and capable of learning.

In the technological whirlwind of contemporary society, it is a challenge to find the quiet spaces in our schools and other institutions, so that we may find vital time to reflect together on the meaning and impact of our professional activities upon the lives of the children and adults we serve. We can meet the challenge if we choose to work on ourselves and if we choose to view our institutions as formed by humans and capable of being reformed by us.

Bibliography

Acheson, K., & Gall, M. D. (1980). *Techniques in the clinical supervision of teachers: Preservice and inservice applications*. New York: Longman.

Adams, R. D. (1982). Teacher development: A look at changes in teacher perceptions and behavior across time. *The Journal of Teacher Education, 33*(4), 40–43.

Almy, M. (1975). *The early childhood educator at work*. New York: McGraw-Hill.

Almy, M., & Genishi, C. (1979). *Ways of studying children: An observation manual for early childhood teachers* (rev. ed.). New York: Teachers College Press.

Argyris, C., & Schon, D. A. (1975). *Theory in practice: Increasing professional effectiveness*. London: Jossey-Bass.

Bartlett, F. C. (1932). *Remembering: A study in experimental and social psychology*. Cambridge: Cambridge University Press.

Beuf, A. H. (1979). *Biting off the bracelet: A study of children in hospitals*. Philadelphia: University of Pennsylvania Press.

Bloomfield, D. (1976). Perspectives on teaching. (Doctoral dissertation, Union College Graduate School).

Blumer, H. (1969). *Symbolic interactionism: Perspective and method*. Englewood Cliffs, NJ: Prentice-Hall.

Blythe, R. (1969). *Akenfield: Portrait of an English village*. New York: Pantheon Books.

Bronfenbrenner, U. (1979). *The ecology of human development: Experiments by nature and design*. Cambridge: Harvard University Press.

Brophy, J., & Evertson, C. (1976). *Learning from teaching: A developmental perspective*. Boston: Allyn & Bacon.

Brown, M. W. (1947). *Goodnight moon*. New York: Harper & Row.

Bruner, J. S. (1960). *The process of education*. Cambridge, MA: Harvard University Press.

Bucher, R., & Stelling, J. G. (1977). *Becoming a professional*. Beverly Hills, CA: Sage.

Bussis, A. M., Chittenden, E. A., & Amarel, M. (1976). *Beyond surface curriculum: An interview study of teachers' understandings*. Boulder, CO: Westview.

Butterfield, F. (1981, January 5). How China raises its well-behaved children. *The New York Times*, p. B10.

Carini, P. F. (1982). *The school lives of seven children: A five year study*. Grand Forks, ND: University of North Dakota Press.

Cassirer, E. (1970). *An essay on man: An introduction to a philosophy of human culture*. New York: Bantam Books.

Chukovsky, K. (1971). *From two to five* (rev. ed.) (M. Morton, trans.). Berkeley, CA: University of California Press.

Cohen, D., & Stern, V. (1978). *Observing and recording the behavior of young children* (rev. ed.). New York: Teachers College Press.

Dewey, J. (1960). *The child and the curriculum* and *The School and society* (rev. ed.). Chicago: University of Chicago Press.

Dilthey, W. (1977). *Descriptive psychology and historical understanding*. The Hague: Nijhoff.

Eisner, E. (1979). *The educational imagination: On the design and evaluation of school programs*. New York: Macmillan.

Elbaz, F. (1981). The teacher's "practical knowledge": Report of a case study. *Curriculum Inquiry, 11*, 43–71.

Erickson, F. (1979). Mere ethnography: Some problems in its use in educational practice. *Anthropology and Education Quarterly, 10*, 182–188.

Frankl, V. E. (1963). *Man's search for meaning: An introduction to logotherapy* (rev. ed.) (I. Lasch, trans.). New York: Pocket Books.

General Professional Education of the Physician and College Preparation for Medicine Panel. (1984). *Physicians for the twenty-first century*. Washington, DC: Association of American Medical Colleges.

Goldsmith, O. (1902). *The deserted village, a poem*. New York: Harper & Brothers.

Hall, E. (1983). A conversation with Erik Erikson. *Psychology Today, 17*, 22–30.

Hunter, M. (1984). Knowing, teaching, and supervising. In P. L. Hosford (Ed.), *Using what we know about teaching* (pp. 169–193). Alexandria, VA: Association for Supervision and Curriculum Development.

Hyman, R. T. (1980). Fielding student questions. *Theory into Practice, 19*, 38–44.

Isaacs, S. (1930). *Intellectual growth in young children*. London: Routledge & Kegan Paul.

Isaacs, S. (1971). *The children we teach: Seven to eleven years* (rev. ed.). New York: Schocken Books.

Janesick, V. (1982). Of snakes and circles: Making sense of classroom group processes through a case study. *Curriculum Inquiry, 12*(2), 161–190.

Jersild, A. T. (1955). *When teachers face themselves*. New York: Teachers College Press.

Kamii, C. L. (1984). Obedience is not enough. *Young Children, 39*(4), 11–14.

Katz, L. G. (1977). *Talks with teachers: Reflections on early childhood education*. Washington, DC: National Association for the Education of Young Children.

Kessen, W. (1979). The American child and other cultural inventions. *American Psychologist, 34*(10), 815–820.

Krauss, R. (1945). *The carrot seed*. New York: Scholastic Book Services.

Kuh, K. (1979). Clyfford Still. In J. P. O'Neill (Ed.), *Clyfford Still* (pp. 9–19). New York: Harry N. Abrams.

Lortie, D. (1975). *Schoolteacher: A sociological study*. Chicago: University of Chicago Press.

Marshall, S. (1968). *An experiment in education*. Cambridge: Cambridge University Press.

Maslow, A. (1968). *Toward a psychology of being*. Princeton, NJ: D. Van Nostrand.

McDermott, R. P. (1982). Rigor and respect as standards in ethnographic description. *Harvard Educational Review, 52*, 321–328.

McNeil, J. D. (1982). A scientific approach to supervision. In T. J. Sergiovanni (Ed.), *Supervision of teaching* (pp. 18–34).

Washington, DC: Association for Supervision and Curriculum Development.

Mead, M. (1972). *Blackberry winter: My earlier years.* New York: Simon & Schuster.

Miller, J. B. (1976). *Toward a new psychology of women.* Boston: Beacon Press.

Minuchin, P. P. (1977). *The middle years of childhood.* Monterey, CA: Brooks/Cole.

Mitchell, L. S. (1971). *Young geographers: How they explore the world and how they map the world* (rev. ed.). New York: Bank Street College of Education (original work published in 1934).

Olsen, T. (1974). *Yonnondio: From the thirties.* New York: Delacorte Press.

Pratt, C. (1970). *I learn from children.* New York: Cornerstone Library.

Reid, W. A. (1979). Practical reasoning and curriculum theory: In search of a new paradigm. *Curriculum Inquiry, 9*(3), 187–208.

Sarason, S. B. (1971). *The culture of school and the problem of change.* Boston: Allyn & Bacon.

Sartre, J. P. (1964). *The words.* Greenwich, CT: Fawcett.

Schactel, E. G. (1968). On memory and childhood amnesia. In T. Talbot (Ed.), *The world of the child: Birth to adolescence from the child's viewpoint* (pp. 10–52). New York: J. Aronson (original work published in 1947).

Schön, D. A. (1983). *The reflective practitioner: How professionals think in action.* New York: Basic Books.

Smith, L. M., & Geoffrey, W. (1968). *The complexities of an urban classroom: An analysis toward a general theory of teaching.* New York: Holt, Rinehart & Winston.

Spodek, B. (1985). *Teaching in the early years* (3rd ed.). Englewood Cliffs, NJ: Prentice-Hall.

Spradley, J. P. (1979). *The ethnographic interview.* New York: Holt, Rinehart & Winston.

Terkel, S. (1980). *American dreams: Lost and found.* New York: Pantheon Books.

Valverde, L. A. (1982). The self-evolving supervisor. In T. J. Sergiovanni (Ed.), *Supervision of teaching* (pp. 81–90).

Washington, DC: Association for Supervision and Curriculum Development.

Wann, K. D., Dorn, M. S., & Liddle, E. A. (1970). *Fostering intellectual development in young children* (6th ed.). New York: Teachers College Press.

Withall, J. (1967). Anthology of classroom observation instruments. In A. Simon and E. G. Boyer (Eds.), *Mirrors for behavior* (pp. 4–8). Philadelphia: Research for Better Schools.

Woolf, V. (1976). *Moments of being.* New York: Harcourt Brace Jovanovich.

Yonemura, M. (1977). Overcoming deficit thinking in teacher education. In B. Spodek (Ed.), *Teaching practices: Reexamining assumptions* (pp. 57–63). Washington, DC: National Association for the Education of Young Children.

Yonemura, M. (1980). How children teach us. *Today's Education, 69*(1), 59–68.

Yonemura, M. (1982). Teacher conversations: A potential source of their own professional growth. *Curriculum Inquiry, 12*(3), 239–256.

Index

About the Author
and the Participants

Margaret V. Yonemura was a social worker, then a teacher and director in schools for young children before entering the field of teacher education. She earned her B.Sc. degree at the University of London, and her M.A. and Ed.D. degrees at Teachers College, Columbia University. Prior to her appointment as a professor of education at the State University of New York at Binghamton, she was chairperson of graduate programs at Bank Street College of Education. Her research centers on professional development and the education of young children.

Jean Acosta-Colletti received degrees in early childhood education, including an A.S. from Nassau Community College and a B.S. from Trenton State College. She completed her master's degree at S.U.N.Y.–Binghamton, and taught young children for eight years before entering a doctoral program in early childhood education at Indiana University at Bloomington.

Jeffrey Collins graduated from Harpur College, S.U.N.Y.–Binghamton, with a B.A. in Psychology, and completed a Master of Science in Education, also at S.U.N.Y.–Binghamton. He is currently the science specialist at the Susquehanna School in Binghamton, where he works with children from two through fourteen years.